OUR⌃TOWN

Old

OUR ∧ TOWN

The History of a Neighborhood

SHIRLEY BAUGHER

Four boys, Chicago, 1871

The Old Town Triangle Association

Credits

PHOTO RESEARCH	Carolyn Blackmon
PHOTO CAPTIONS	Carolyn Blackmon and Shirley Baugher
PHOTO RESEARCH	Carolyn Blackmon
PHOTO EDITING	Carolyn Blackmon and Norman Baugher
HISTORIC PHOTO SOURCES	Chicago Historical Society, Old Town Triangle Association
DESIGN & PRODUCTION	Norman Baugher
COVER PAINTING	Norman Zimmerman
EDITING & PROOFREADING	Trinda Gray O'Connor
PRINTING	Chicago Press Corporation

COVER PAINTING:
OLD TOWN HOUSES BUILT BY CHARLES WEYER
AT 229-31 W. EUGENIE IN 1874 BEFORE FRAME
HOUSES WERE OUTLAWED WITHIN THE CITY
LIMITS.

Library of Congress Catalogue Card Number: pfs22557

ISBN 0-9672296-1-8

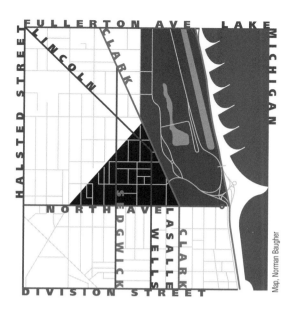

Map, Norman Baugher

CONTENTS

PERFORMANCE BY GEN. GEORGE BELL, JR.,
POST 150, 1939-41, VFW BAND
EUGENIE, CLARK, & LASALLE STREETS

PREFACE

THIS IS A BOOK about a neighborhood. In the grand scheme of things, it is not a famous, or even an infamous, neighborhood. Abe Lincoln did not sleep here, but he gave his name to the former resting-place of many of our first settlers. We have no single residence that approaches the architectural triumph of the Glessner House, Henry H. Richardson's urban residential masterpiece at 1800 S. Prairie Avenue (1885-87); or even the Henry B. Clarke House, constructed for the ages by an unknown architect at 1855 S. Indiana Avenue (1836). Still, the five Louis Sullivan row houses on Lincoln Park West (1884), have stood the test of time, as have the John Boland house at 221 W. Eugenie (1884) and St. Michael's Church (1872). No President, Nobel Prize winner, or Time Magazine Man of the Year was born here. No notorious mobster was shot here. And Carl Sandburg was not thinking of the Old Town Triangle when he dubbed the city hog butcher for the world. On the other hand, a renowned Lincoln scholar and director of the Chicago Historical Society lived here, as did some internationally acclaimed artists, newspaper journalists, and movie entrepreneurs. A beloved children's poet was, no doubt, influenced by the discreet charm of Crilly Court when he wrote, "The little toy dog is covered with dust, but sturdy and staunch he stands." And who would be surprised to learn that a few shady deals were negotiated in the now-defunct old saloon on Wells and Eugenie?

Our Old Town is a neighborhood story, but it goes beyond provincialism because the history of the Old Town Triangle mirrors the history of Chicago—founded, sustained, and advanced by enterprising individuals. The text is not an in-depth sociological or geographical community study, merely a sketch of a neighborhood impacted by the large and small events that constituted urban growth and development in the nineteenth and twentieth centuries.

The list of persons who made this book possible is very long, indeed—from the dedicated little band of neighbors who created the Old Town Triangle Association in 1948 to the current board of directors who keep their vision alive. I especially thank all those who recorded their thoughts about the neighborhood and its activities in the art fair program books from 1950 to the present day. I am pleased to pass along their memories to a new generation. I am grateful to neighbor Diane Gonzalez who collected and referenced many of the sources used in this book and to staff in the Research Department of the Chicago Historical Society who helped me sort through stacks of files and records to find the documents that tell our story. This was no easy task, for while there is a wealth of information about the south side, the west side, and the downtown area, very little has been published about the near north side. Hopefully, this effort will begin to fill that void. My deepest thanks to Norman Zimmerman for allowing me to use his marvelous paintings of Old Town houses, rooftops, and street scenes. And to my friend Carolyn Blackmon who had no idea what she was getting into when she agreed to serve as photo editor for this book. Her determination to find just the right photographs for the text sent her on a nation-wide (and closet-deep) search. The job wasn't over once she found the photos, however. Then, she had to track down sources and get permission to use them. My sincere thanks to Trinda Gray O'Connor for editing the manuscript. Editing is a special talent, and Trinda was very generous with both her time and talent to help me prepare this book for publication. And, finally, thanks to my own Norman who took all the bits and pieces and made them into a beautiful and lasting tribute to a beautiful and lasting community.

SHIRLEY BAUGHER, 2001

217 W. EUGENIE. AUGUSTINE DEODAT TAYLOR INVENTED THE BALLOON FRAME AND BEGAN USING IT IN CHICAGO IN 1833. IT LAUNCHED A WORLD-CLASS ARCHITECTURE BY ELIMINATING THE NEED FOR HEAVY TIMBERS AND PRECISE MORTISING. IT COULD BE EASILY MASS PRODUCED.

Carolyn Blackmon

Welcome To The Old Town Triangle

OLD TOWN is a community. I don't mean a neighborhood, which is merely a separate physical locale and of which there are dozens throughout Chicago. I mean a community in the sense that the common thread of its varied life, the principle of unity in all its diversity, is a kind of shared experience and shared outlook on life that reminds me of a small town, except that it's interwoven with so much that is cosmopolitan and sophisticated in Chicago.

CHRISTOPHER PORTERFIELD,
Neighbor and Time Magazine Correspondent, 1966

The Way We Are

There is a change when you cross the street at North Avenue and walk north on Wells. It is not a change marked by painted signs or physical divisions. It's as much a feeling as a geographical distinction. Suddenly, you find yourself in a neighborhood of small buildings, tree-lined streets, and friendly people who will stop and say Hello! You have entered the Old Town Triangle.

Local guidebooks will tell you that the Old Town Triangle District is an area, located within the City of Chicago, composed of privately and publicly owned property. Its boundaries are Wisconsin Street, Lincoln Avenue, Wells Street, North Avenue, Mohawk Street, and the former Ogden Avenue right of way (map on contents page v).

The Triangle is an attractive community whose historic buildings and homes are protected by landmark designation (granted in 1977). Under this protection, residents are assured that facades (visible from the street) will not be changed; buildings will not be demolished without express approval of the Landmarks Commission, new construction will not be erected without plans having been approved by the Commission, and signs or billboards will not be placed on or adjacent to landmarks property.

The spirit of the Triangle derives from the Old Town Triangle Association (OTTA), a local organization of approximately 600 residents and families dedicated to the environmental and educational enhancement of the community. Sooner or later, most neighbors drop by the Triangle Center at 1763 N. North Park to voice a concern or get the neighborhood news: who's moved in (or out), what's on the market (and for what price), and which residents are planning rehabs?

The alderman's office records approximately 3,600 registered voters in the Old Town Triangle. While that figure does not present a complete demographic picture, it does give an indication of the number of persons age 21 and over who call the Triangle home at the beginning of the 21st century.

Our Children—Our Future

Old Town is a child-friendly community. Parks and playgrounds dot the landscape and the sound of children playing is a familiar one. Serving the Triangle are two excellent public elementary schools. The LaSalle Language Academy is an Options for Knowledge School specializing in foreign language instruction. Students citywide may apply to LaSalle, which has an enrollment of approximately 600. Lincoln Elementary School features a basic curriculum following Chicago Academic Standards and accepts all neighborhood

ICHi-26843, Photographer, Harold S. Beach

LASALLE SCHOOL, EAST FACADE, 1950

Carolyn Blackmon

children of elementary school age. The local Chicago public secondary school is Lincoln Park High School, which boasts an exemplary general curriculum and an acclaimed International Baccalaureate program. The Latin School of Chicago, a distinguished elementary and high school located at North Avenue and Clark Street, provides an alternative for those parents seeking private school education for their children.

Our Kind of Old Town

Asked to characterize the most outstanding feature of the Triangle community, one long-time resident responded stability. People who come to Old Town as singles tend to marry, put down roots, and raise their children here. When the nest is empty, those not tempted by warmer climates remain because of everything this small corner of the world has to offer.

Coffee shops with tables, either in the windows or outside depending on the season, are found on almost every corner. People greet one another, sit together, discuss the state of the world, or just watch the passing parade—rather like a Left Bank on the Lake. Almost every type of service is available: dental, chiropractic, dry cleaning, real estate, and floral. Walgreens fills prescriptions; McDonalds satisfies guilty fast food cravings. The local bakery is superb. The shops are small and accommodating. Restaurants, a supermarket, a gourmet food store, and a theater complex contribute to the satisfaction of living in this beautiful, old community.

As neighbor Jane Schnedeker put it in 1962, [Old Towners] "are like most other people. Perhaps we've looked a little longer and worked a little harder to find what we want, or maybe, we've just been luckier. We all arrived here for the same reason—we like the peace and quiet, the trees and grass, the freedom to quietly be ourselves. This is our common bond. We go to the festivals of the Buddhist Temple and enjoy ourselves and ask for the teriyaki recipe. We go to church suppers at the Congregational church and come out well-fed and happy. We count the hours and are lulled to sleep by St. Michael's bells. In the summer, we loan garden hoses to our neighbors when it's their turn to water the flowering crab trees. We stop whatever we are doing to trot halfway down the block and admire a neighbor's dog or cat or baby. We consult with each other about ordering firewood in the fall, and in the winter we hibernate, only to rush out when spring arrives to greet the newcomers who have moved in while we were indoors."

This is Old Town in a nutshell. But there is much more to tell. There is the fascinating story of how we got to be who we are, and to learn that, we must take a trip in time back to the mid-nineteenth century.

ADOBO GRILL SIDEWALK CAFE, 1610 N. WELLS ST., 2000.
SECOND CITY CAN BE SEEN IN THE BACKGROUND

Part One

CHAPTER ONE

CHICAGO IN 1830s

Original Town Incorporated Aug.5, 1833

Original City Incorporated Mar.4, 1837

Current Chicago city limits

IN THE BEGINNING

Way Up Yonder in the Cabbage Patch—Chicago and Old Town

A long time ago, when Chicago was very young (1833), what we now call Old Town was only a muddy marshland north of the business district crossed by a ten-mile ditch that carried flood waters from Evanston to the Chicago River. As the marshland dried up, and Chicago stretched northward towards Fullerton Avenue, a group of Roman Catholic immigrants from southern Germany found their way to the north side. They had left behind the cultural and religious restrictions of the Old World and migrated to the American heartland. Mainly farmers and semi-skilled workers, they settled west of Clark Street near the factories on the Chicago River. Almost immediately, they began to establish the institutions that characterize a community: medical facilities, service businesses, schools, fraternal organizations, and a place of worship. In 1846, they built St. Joseph's Church at Chicago and Wabash Avenues.

     In the migratory spirit of nineteenth century American frontiersmen, the German settlers moved northward and continued to expand their holdings by planting the meadows above North Avenue. They con-

LADIES ON THE
STEPS AT
1831 N. ORLEANS,
(97 HAMMOND
STREET), C. 1905.
PROBABLY BUILT
1874, FRAME
CONSTRUCTION
OUTLAWED IN
CITY LIMITS AFTER
1874.

ICHi-26872, Photographer: unknown

verted the dried-up swampland into cow pastures and truck gardens for growing potatoes, cabbages, and celery, and designated the area the Cabbage Patch. Some of what they grew was used for home consumption; the rest was sold to satisfy the hunger of a growing urban population.

Old Town's first houses were small, single family cottages, often no more than twenty by thirty feet. They were constructed by local masons who adopted an inexpensive, balloon framing method that became known as the Chicago Style. The process involved pounding machine manufactured nails into pre-cut boards (two-by-fours) to form rectangular balloon frames and placing them on log bases or brick foundations that served as raised basements. They covered the frame with pine clapboards and topped the entire structure with a pitched roof whose gables faced the front and rear. On the first floor, they stored coal and vegetables. The entry porch and living quarters were on the second floor, which was accessed by a steep set of stairs, a configuration that is still a prominent feature of many Triangle residences. Most of the houses were surrounded by gardens and flowerbeds and had barns in the rear.

We Gather Together

Until mid-century, Cabbage Patch parishioners continued to worship at St. Joseph's Church. As the north side population grew, however, residents felt the need for a neighborhood parish. In 1852, Michael Diversey, part owner of the Diversey and Lill brewery and a prominent member of St.

Joseph's, donated a plot of land at North and Hudson Avenues for a church. In four months, local builders completed a 40– by 60-foot frame building with a single bell in the cupola. The finished building cost $730 and was dedicated to St. Michael, Mr. Diversey's patron saint.

Michael Diversey owned other large tracts of land on the north side which were annexed by the City of Chicago in the early 1850s, extending Chicago's northern boundary to what is now Fullerton Avenue. The availability of this property within the city limits attracted a number of prosperous and politically prominent citizens. William B. Ogden, Chicago's first mayor, came in 1856, as did William Rand and Andrew McNally, who later gained fame as map publishers. Irish, Italian and French immigrants joined the established German population and enriched the Cabbage Patch with their talents as shoemakers, tailors, brewers, carpenters, railroad workers, and grain elevator operators.

OLD TOWN ROOFTOPS, 1708-1714 N. CRILLY COURT WITH CRILLY APARTMENTS IN THE BACKGROUND- SEEN FROM FOURTH FLOOR DECK OF NORTH PARK CONDOMINIUMS.

Norman Zimmerman

Like the rest of the city, the community was experiencing tremendous economic and social growth. Under Mayor Ogden's enthusiastic leadership, the first swing bridge built over the Chicago River allowed inhabitants to move more freely from one part of the city to another. Ogden promoted the building of miles of railroads which enabled farmers to get their produce to other markets, as did the Illinois and Michigan Canal and the Chicago and Michigan Steam Boat Company. The razing of a red light district just to the south of the Cabbage Patch made the area a more desirable place to live; and investments in businesses like the Diversey and Lill Brewery added to the area's prosperity.

By 1869, St. Michael's burgeoning parish could not be contained in the existing tiny church. Enterprising parishioners established a new site at Cleveland and Eugenie Streets and put up a much larger facility with a school, a convent, and a home for priests. The new complex cost $130,000—178 times the amount of the original little church.

First hand accounts from persons living in the Cabbage Patch in the 1850s are not easy to come by, but there is an interesting description written by a portrait artist from Paris, G.P.A. Healy in 1855. Mr. Healy came to Chicago from Paris as the guest of Mayor William B. Ogden whose enthusiasm for the city was infectious. Living in the mayor's north side residence for a brief period, Healy painted a number of Ogden's friends. During his tenure he wrote: "Chicago was like an overgrown youth whose legs and arms are too long for his clothes and who scarcely knows how to dispose of his lank, awkward body. The city stretched along the lake shore and into the prairie–unfinished, ragged, uncouth. The streets were abominably paved. The sidewalks, raised high above the level of the streets, were composed of rough planks, often out of repair so that one had to pick ones way very carefully for fear of accidents. Big nails seemed placed there on purpose to catch in the women's dresses. The mud was so deep in bad weather that from side to side, rickety boards served as unsafe bridges and the unfortunate horses waded laboriously along as best they could. The most enormous rats scurried under the sidewalks, and uncouth shanties raised their shabby heads close to fine new mansions."

Such conditions did not discourage Healy, however. Though he returned to Paris after his visit, he could not get Chicago out of his mind. When his wife died, he came back to the midwestern metropolis, opened a studio, and continued to paint until his death.

From Resting Place to Recreation Space

For a few decades after Chicago was founded, the land to the north and east of the Cabbage Patch was used as a cemetery. The City Council had selected the area as a burial site because of its great distance from the city's original northern boundary (Kinzie Street). In 1844, North Side Alderman Lawrence Proudfoot decided that residents of his ward would be better served by a recreation site than a cemetery, and he began a crusade to have the graves removed from what was then called The City Cemetery. He was supported by public health reformers who were conducting a campaign against unsanitary burial practices. Mr. Proudfoot's

COUCH MAUSOLEUM AT THE SOUTH END OF
LINCOLN PARK. ONE OF TWO GRAVESITES
NOT DUG UP AND MOVED OUTSIDE THE
CITY LIMITS IN 1864.

Carolyn Blackmon

protest lasted twenty years, but in 1864, his efforts were finally rewarded. The municipal cemetery was closed, and the Council passed an ordinance forbidding the sale of any further cemetery lots. At the same time, aldermen approved a plan to relocate the existing graves to the suburban areas of Graceland, Rosehill, and Oak Woods. Though outside the city limits, the relocated cemeteries were easily accessible to residents via Chicago's improved transportation system: a steam railroad commuter service, a horse-drawn street railway system, and a span bridge over the river at Rush Street, publicized as the first iron bridge west of the Alleghenies. The original cemetery site was decreed a park and was named after the assassinated President Abraham Lincoln.

Today, Old Town residents and visitors can still visit two monuments from the old City Cemetery. Ira Couch and his family are buried in a large mausoleum at the southern end of the park near the Chicago Historical Society. Couch, owner of one of the city's leading hotels, the Tremont House on the southeast corner of Lake and Dearborn Streets, built the mausoleum and had the family name carved above the door. The tomb remains because the Illinois Supreme Court supported the family's refusal to move the monument.

Just inside the entrance to Lincoln Park, at the foot of Wisconsin Street, stands a granite boulder that marked the potter's field section of the cemetery. The man whose grave it designates was probably the most historically prominent person ever buried there, David Kennison. Mr. Kennison, who died in 1852 at the age of 115, was the last survivor of the Boston Tea Party. He was present when Cornwallis surrendered at Yorktown to end the Revolutionary War and was still on active duty at age 75 after having fought in more than seven battles of the War of 1812.

DAVID KENNISON BOULDER MARKING
THE ENTRANCE TO THE POTTER'S
FIELD SECTION OF THE OLD CITY
CEMETERY AT WISCONSIN AND CLARK
STREETS. THE CEMETERY CLOSED IN
1864 AND GRAVES REMOVED OUTSIDE
THE CITY LIMITS.

Carolyn Blackmon

FIRE ENGINE, 1871. MODEL OF THE
FREDERICK GUND FROM COMPANY
14, USED IN THE GREAT CHICAGO
FIRE

C H A P T E R   T W O

INFERNO

ICHi-02665

ONE COLD NIGHT while we were all in bed
Old Mother Leary left the lantern in the shed.
And when the cow kicked it over, he clicked his heels and said
There'll be a hot time in the Old Town tonight.

Mrs. O'Leary's Who Did What?
Old Town and The Great Chicago Fire

Tragedy struck Chicago and the Cabbage Patch in 1871 with the outbreak of the Great Fire, arguably the greatest disaster of its kind in American history. Given the construction materials of streets and buildings in that period, one could almost have predicted the fire. The city had 55 miles of planked streets. Wooden bridges formed the passages across rivers and canals. Roofs were made of tar and pine chips—both highly flammable, and large quantities of hay and straw were kept in the city as feed for horses.

Though Chicago had an excellent 185-man fire department, its steam-powered water pumpers were only a little more effective than the old bucket brigades. Then, as now, the key to fighting fires effectively was rapid response to alarms. To assure that calls were answered quickly, watchmen situated high in the cupola over the courthouse kept a 24-hour

CHS, ICHi-02881-9, engraving of sketch by Theodore Davis

lookout. Each department also had an observation tower. When watchmen spotted flames, they notified firehouses of the location.

Had this system been working effectively when the Great Fire broke out, it might have been contained in a small area, despite the fact that the wooden buildings and streets covering much of the city were dried out by a blisteringly hot summer in which little rain had fallen. But the system wasn't working.

On Saturday, October 7, a terrible fire started in a planing mill on Canal Street between Jackson and Van Buren Streets. It took nearly one hundred firefighters fifteen hours to extinguish the blaze, which spread over four city blocks. Several of the engines and hose carts were so badly damaged they could not be used without extensive repairs. To make matters worse, after all those hours of nonstop exertion, more than half the city's firefighters were unfit for duty. And the worst was yet to come.

Legend has it that the Great Chicago Fire started when Mrs. O'Leary's cow kicked over the lantern in her barn. Maybe—and maybe not. Contemporary accounts agree that the fire did start on October 8, 1871, in one of the outbuildings on the O'Leary's property at 137 DeKoven Street. No one is quite sure about the part played by the cow. Speculation about the cause includes lightning, raucous tenants, a drunken neighbor, and, of course, the cantankerous cow. However it happened, the fire broke out early on the evening of the eighth and burned for 20 minutes before the first watchman turned in an alarm, but that alarm failed to reg-

RELIC HOUSE, 1872-1929, WAS BUILT WITH MATERIALS SALVAGED FROM THE FIRE. THIS POPULAR BEER GARDEN AND MUSEUM STOOD ON CLARK STREET ACROSS FROM LINCOLN PARK.

ister. By the time another watchman in a distant fire tower saw the flames and dispatched his company to the site, the fire had been raging for 30 minutes and had spread to the adjacent buildings.

Other companies began to respond, but seven were dispatched to wrong locations. When they finally arrived at the actual site, the fire was out of control. By 2:30 a.m. Monday, fed by southwest winds, the inferno had jumped the Chicago River and was roaring northward.

With the exception of the Water Tower and pumping station at Chicago Avenue and Pine Street (Michigan Avenue), most of the North District, including the Cabbage Patch, was covered by small wooden shops and cottages. (The Water Tower survived the flames; the pumping station did not, and the City lost its water supply.) The new Chicago Historical Society at Dearborn and Ontario, said to be the most fireproof building in the city, burned to the ground in 30 minutes. The Mahlon Ogden (brother of Mayor William B. Ogden) mansion, which stood on the site of the current Newberry Library on Walton and Dearborn Streets was saved; but Ogden's neighbor, Ezra B. McCogg, watched his home go up in flames. Interestingly, not one window in Mr. McCogg's greenhouse was broken.

As the fire spread through the north side, one Chicagoan recalled, "You couldn't see anything over you but fire—no sky, no clouds, no stars, nothing but fire." It was like a tornado of fire. Looters plundered goods from deserted stores. Bridges collapsed under the weight of hundreds of persons running for their lives. One woman knelt in the street with a crucifix before her face only to be hit by a runaway truck. Household possessions loaded onto trucks were burning as the drivers sped to safety. Masses huddled in the shallow water along the lake shore; others found shelter in the empty graves of the old City Cemetery at the south end of Lincoln Park. Flames created temperatures so high that plate glass windows cracked, iron and steel melted, and limestone construction blocks disintegrated.

As the fire approached St. Michael's, the bells began to toll. Parishioners gathered outside, confident that their church, which was built of brick and stone, would stand. When they saw the Alexian Hospital go up in flames, however, they began to remove the church's treasures: the large wooden crucifix, Bibles, candelabra, statues, and altar pieces and buried them in the monastery grounds. Nuns and priests loaded the hand-carved stations of the cross, vestments, and altar cloths onto a wagon and sent them to safety at Rosehill, outside the city limits.

The fire was not brought under control until the evening of October 9th. Since there were so few buildings north of Fullerton, there was nothing left to burn. A heavy rain began to fall during the night, and by Tuesday morning, October 10th, the fire was out, except for some coal piles and heaps of rubble, which smoldered for months.

In three days, the fire had destroyed an area of more than three square miles—from Taylor Street north to Fullerton and west to the Chicago River. At its height, flames were seen as far away as DesPlaines, 20 miles from Chicago. More than one-third of the city was devastated, including 17,450 structures, mostly on the north side. The entire downtown—department stores, wholesale warehouses, Board of Trade, and hotels—was destroyed in one night. Over one million dollars in currency, presumably protected by three inches of boiler plate and a wall of brick in the Post Office and Custom House, was incinerated in the fire's 3,000 degree heat. The same was true of currency in the city's banks. At least 300 people died and 90,000 were left homeless. Ironically, Mrs. O'Leary's cottage, south of the cow barn, was undamaged.

St. Michael's walls survived the fire; but the interior was destroyed, along with the altar fixtures and statues that the parishioners had buried. Even the huge bells dropped from the tower and melted in the intense heat. Gone too were the school, the sisters' convent, and the priests' home.

2121 N. HUDSON, FORMER HOME OF RICHARD BELLINGER AND THE ONLY HOME ON THE NORTH SIDE TO SURVIVE THE GREAT FIRE OF 1871.

Carolyn Blackmon

For weeks, relief carts carrying bread and meat moved through the Cabbage Patch and up Armitage as far as Central Street where debris kept them from going further. Within the community, only the Hanselman family managed to save anything. The chairs and doors, which they had buried in a hole in the backyard, were found intact, and were used to furnish their new home at 1814 N. Orleans. Mr. Hanselman's favorite black walnut arm chair took its accustomed spot in the front room.

The only north side residence left standing, other than Ogden's, was a frame cottage in the 2100 block of Lincoln Place (now Hudson Avenue) belonging to a newly married policeman named Richard Bellinger. Bellinger had recently built the small white house for his wife and desperately wanted to save it. He raked up all the dry leaves in his yard and ripped up the wooden sidewalk, picket fence, and the front steps. He covered his roof with blankets and rugs and propped a ladder against the side of the house. Then, he and his brother-in-law set up a bucket brigade bringing water from nearby wells and ditches and wetting down the roof. The two men battled the embers which landed on the roof all night long, but they saved the house. Today, a plaque on the front facade commemorates the house's survival.

CHAPTER THREE

STARTING OVER

O
N THREE SCORE SPIRES *had sunset shone*
Where ghastly sunrise looked on none.
Men clasped each other's hands, and said:
"The City of the West is dead!"

A COMMUNITY REBUILDS
JOHN GREENLEAF WHITTIER

Chicago was not dead. It was a phoenix, about to rise from the ashes. True, the downtown and many residential areas were destroyed, but Chicago's essential infrastructure was not. Most of the grain elevators remained, as did the lumber district, stockyards, and factories located outside the burn area. Even more important, the City's railway network was virtually intact. In the first post-fire edition published by the *Chicago Tribune*, citizens were urged to "CHEER UP. In the midst of calamity without parallel in the world's history, looking upon the ashes of thirty years accumulations," wrote the editors, "the people of this once beautiful city have resolved that CHICAGO SHALL RISE AGAIN!"

Relief poured in from the Fire and Aid Relief Society to help the homeless and to rebuild residential areas. The main flow of capital came from investors and from the mercantile and business interests throughout the world: New York, St. Louis, Washington D.C., Paris, and London.

The British gave 8,000 books for a public library. Actors gave benefit performances and sportsmen played benefit games. Chicago had become too important in the economic life of the United States and Europe to allow it to fail. Within two years, the city had been completely rebuilt.

There were some who said that the Great Fire had actually done more good than harm by producing a phenomenal construction boom and driving up the price of Chicago real estate. With the destruction of the old wooden structures, businessmen and homeowners rebuilt using the latest techniques for fire prevention. The building boom was so widespread that one historian wrote, "It is common to see ten, a dozen, or fifty houses rising at once; but when one looks upon ten thousand houses rising and ten times that number of busy workmen coming and going, and listens to the noise of countless saws and hammer, and chisels, and axes, and planes, he is bewildered."

Architects designed taller office buildings to produce more rent given the expensive property on which they stood in the downtown area. Constructed of masonry over iron and steel frameworks, the new buildings were labeled skyscrapers . By the time of the Chicago World's' Fair in 1893, the city had become famous for the height of its downtown office

Norman Zimmerman

buildings. Men like William LeBaron Jenny, John Wellborn Root, Dankmar Adler, Martin Roche, William Holabird, Louis Sullivan, and Daniel Burnham became the leaders of the Chicago School of Architecture.

Nothing exemplifies the energy with which Chicagoans approached the restitution of their city more than the rebuilding of St. Michael's Church. The rubble had no sooner been cleared than parishioners began restoration. As a temporary measure, they propped a 90-foot wooden shanty against the surviving stone wall in the church garden. One week later, priests were conducting services in this makeshift shelter. By November, local carpenters had erected another building which was used as both church and school until damage to the main building was repaired (at a cost of $40,000). The new building was then used exclusively as a school. On October 12, 1872, one year after the fire, a dedication ceremony was held for the renovated and refurbished church. The next year, parishioners held a big parade to celebrate St. Michael's resurrection. Marching bands from parishes citywide met at Erie Street and walked two miles north to the church doors. They stopped before a huge wreath inscribed with gold letters: "Welcome you, friends from far and near, To bless this, the house of our Lord most dear." The bells were not returned until 1876. There were five of them, cast in bronze by the McShane Company. They were named after St. Michael, St. Mary, St. Joseph, St. Alphonsus, and St. Theresa.

Fearing the outbreak of another fire, some families left Chicago. Most remained and rebuilt their homes, often on the ashes of the old. Assisted by the Fire Relief & Aid Society, residents were able to build new houses quickly and cheaply using the Chicago balloon-frame style. The houses could be constructed at a location where materials were easily accessible and moved by wagon to a burned-out lot.

In 1874, the City Council passed an ordinance outlawing construction of nonmasonry buildings within the city limits (roughly as far north as Fullerton Avenue). Thousands of north side residents who could not afford to rebuild in brick were forced to sell their lots and move just over the northern border where developers were only too eager to provide inexpensive wooden houses for them. The contrast between the nonmasonry part of the city and the wooden suburbs can still be seen along Fullerton Avenue west of Halsted.

The appearance and constituency of the Cabbage Patch changed after the Fire. Wealthy families from the south and west sides of the city moved into the area and commissioned brick and stone mansions and town houses, usually in Queen Anne or Italianate style. Often, these more elaborate structures were built on lots adjacent to humbler brick and balloon-frame cottages, adding to diversity of the neighborhood. With this diversity came a new designation. The Cabbage Patch was renamed North Town.

In the Gloaming

By the end of the nineteenth century, Germans, Scots, Hungarians, Italians, Irish, Assyrians, Filipinos, Greeks, and Japanese had moved into North Town and lived side by side in houses that, though densely packed, still managed to maintain fairly large lawns and orchards. They rode the same public transportation to the Loop, a long, cold ride in winter via horse-drawn car; their children shared the Swan Ride in Lincoln Park (for five cents a trip); and many cycled together in the Lincoln Cycling Club on the present site of the Lincoln Hotel. The lamplighter made his rounds at twilight. People kept chickens in their yards, and fed grass to the cows kept in a pasture on Sedgwick. The milk from these cows was poured into large metal cans and sold door to door.

CHAPTER FOUR

BOOM YEARS

No Business Like Old Town Business

The growth of the Chicago business community after the Great Fire, was mirrored by business development in the Old Town area in the 1870s and 80s. At North Avenue and Wells stood Piper's Bakery with its imposing facade and magnificent Victorian interior. Piper's, which had begun as a modest mom and pop operation before the Fire (he baked the bread and she sold it door to door), grew into a major enterprise employing more than 500 people and shipping its products to 39 states. Next to the bakery was the Fick and Schute Private School, which, according to resident Leo Weissenborn, graduated many prominent citizens. Among them were Felix Riesenberg who was a member of Walter Wellman's expedition to the North Pole where he stayed for an entire winter alone with the equipment and dogs. Riesenberg later wrote a best seller called *East Side — West Side*. Elise Schumm Berwick became a physician and did post graduate medical work in Zurich. Dr. Berwick's brother, also a Fick and Schute graduate, attended West Point and became a colonel in the U. S. Army. He is buried in Arlington Cemetery next to Admiral Perry.

Around the corner, at 410 North Avenue, was a shoe store opened in 1881 by Henry Brandt. It was still going strong in the 1950s under the management of Brandt's son and grandsons. George and Emma Heller Schumm had an office on North Avenue where they edited The Alliance, a weekly newspaper founded by the Reverend George C. Miln. (Mr. Schumm later went on to Boston as an editor on The Nation magazine.) Further down was a popular antique trunk store that catered to the needs of a population now able to move beyond its neighborhood confines.

Begun in the late nineteenth century and prospering well into the twentieth century were two companies that produced alcoholic beverages: the Recher Wine and Liquor Company opened at 332 North Avenue in 1890, and the Peter Hand Brewing Company was founded in the 1890s by the eponymous Peter Hand and partners John Heuer and Dr. Joseph Watry. The Peter Hand brewery distributes Meister Brau beer throughout the Midwest to this day. The Brewer's Digest noted in a 1963 article called Beer and Urban Renewal, that two of Old Town's most prestigious houses were built for brewers: the Frederick Wacker home in 1872 and the Francis J. Dewes house in 1896.

Halcyon Days

During the glory days of the 1890s, sight-seeing carriages picked up tourists at the Germania Club and drove them through the business and residential districts of North Town. Newspapermen, writers, artists, lawyers, and manufacturers came through and liked what they saw. Many bought property in the neighborhood and built two- and three-story homes. Among the newcomers was Eugene Field, a poet and columnist for the *Chicago Daily News* (later *The Record*) who took up residence on Crilly Court where he wrote his children's classic Little Boy Blue and Wynken,

WYNKEN, BLYNKEN, & NOD STATUE IN LINCOLN PARK COMMEMORATING FORMER RESIDENT, POET EUGENE FIELD. FIELD WROTE THE BELOVED CHILDREN'S POEM DURING TENURE ON CRILLY COURT. *SO SHUT YOUR EYES WHILE MOTHER SINGS OF WONDERFUL SIGHTS THAT BE, AND YOU SHALL SEE THE BEAUTIFUL THINGS AS YOU ROCK IN THE MISTY SEA, WHERE THE OLD SHOE ROCKED THE FISHERMEN THREE: WYNKEN, BLYNKEN, AND NOD.*

Carolyn Blackmon

Blynken, and Nod. This structure later became known as the Wynken, Blynken, and Nod house.

North Town was an important transportation hub for the City. The North Chicago City Railway built huge stables on Orleans Street where LaSalle School now stands. They had to be big because the NCRR used 1,500 horses to draw its 250 cars. A repair shop for the carriages was constructed at Eugenie and North Park.

Manufacturing played a prominent part in the thriving economy of the area. The first large factory to come in was the Deering Harvester Company, a manufacturer of farm equipment. South of the horse car barns, in a Gold Leaf factory owned by the Schwartz family, workers flattened hunks of gold with copper-covered mallets. The Cheyney brothers bought looms and established a prosperous silk factory on the northwest corner of Eugenie and North Park. Just east of LaSalle School, where the Orleans House apartments now stand, was the Fiedler Silk and Wool Factory, built in 1914 to manufacture buttons and dress ornaments. Another fabric company, Baum's Silk Mills was located on Blackhawk Street.

Other manufacturing establishments on the north side included the Western Wheel Works on Schiller, Oscar Mayer on Sedgwick, and a soap factory on North Avenue between North Park and Sedgwick. A short distance away, there was an ice house that sold to both domestic and commercial establishments. Heavier industries were located west of Halsted Street. Standing in the Newberry School yard on any given day, one could hear 200 factory whistles announcing the start, lunch break, and end of the working day.

The streets in 1890s North Town would be recognizable to contemporary residents, but many of their names would not. Armitage, for example, was Center Street. Lincoln Park West was North Park, North Park was North Franklin, Orleans was Hammond, St. Paul was Florimond, Willow was Tell Court, and Concord was Starr Street. At the century's close, the last four streets had not been paved.

THE KOENIGSBERG SALOON,
CHARLEY'S, WAS BUILT IN THE 1870S
AS A FEED STORE AND SALOON, THIS
WAS ONE OF OLD TOWN'S MOST
POPULAR WATERING HOLES FOR
MANY YEARS.

CHAPTER FIVE

A TAVERN IN THE TOWN

ICHi-04870 Photographer unknown

Chicago has always been a great saloon city (about one saloon to every sixty families) and Old Town has had its share of popular taverns. In North Town, the saloon was more than just a place to buy a beer or a shot. It was a community center where neighbors got together and shared news and concerns. The barkeep or owner often served as an ear for family troubles, a banker to lend money to patrons who were down on their luck, and an employment service to hook up workers and employers. There were ethnic newspapers available for those who could not read English and a quick sandwich for factory workers during the noon break. The neighborhood's favorite drinking establishment was located on the southwest corner of Wells and Eugenie. Built in the 1870s, C. H. Nieman and Company was a combination feed store and saloon. Farmers who drove their carts from the agricultural areas north of Fullerton Avenue would arrive during the early morning and buy feed for their stock. Afterwards, they would stop next door to discuss the news and take liquid refreshment.

The feed store/tavern was then sold to Mr. C. Koenigsberg who added charming Victorian gingerbread features to the facade and established a family residence on the second floor. His children Walter (who later moved to 1707 North Park) and Irma (who married Mr. James J. O'Toole and moved to 1706 Crilly Court) were born there.

Both the exterior and interior appointments of the building were in excellent condition when it was purchased by the Zahners—perhaps the most successful of all the owners. Zahners' was well-known throughout the city for its ornate bar, elegant ladies' café, jangly mechanical piano, carved beer steins imported from Europe, and for the portrait of Mayor Carter Harrison which kept a vigilant eye over the merriment of the patrons.

Unfortunately, this venerable establishment deteriorated with age and eventually fell to the wrecker's ball. Edgar Crilly, son of the developer of Crilly Court, purchased the plot in the early 1950s and transformed it into a park with flowers, trees, and shrubs.

Another well-known saloon favored by Old Town residents from the time Prohibition ended to 1967 had a more political flavor. It was the De Luxe Gardens at North Avenue and Sedgwick, which occupied the former premises of the Immigrant State Bank. The De Luxe kept all of the bank's accoutrements—high ceilings, grilles barring the way to the vaults, and imposing marble décor—giving it a rather sedate appearance. Residents didn't just go to this establishment to enjoy a beer or two, however. They went to pass the time with the Alderman of the 43rd Ward Mathias J. (Paddy) Bauler.

There has probably never been a more colorful alderman or a more experienced saloonkeeper than Paddy—nobody called him Mathias. From the time he was old enough, he worked behind the bar in his father's saloon. During Prohibition, he ran a speakeasy at the corner of Willow and Howe Streets where Old Towners rubbed shoulders with entertainers (Rudy Vallee), politicians (Anton Cermak), and socialites (Edith Rockefeller McCormick). Paddy's first political job was as a time-keeper in the Cook County Treasurer's office. He was elected to the City Council as Alderman of the 43rd Ward in 1933, and won every aldermanic race but one for the next 34 years. He used to boast, "Every election comes up and they put some egghead against me. When the election is over, yours truly comes back to the City Council."

The enormously popular Paddy was not Irish, as many thought from his adopted nickname. In fact, his roots had more in common with the neighborhood's original German community. His father was born in Germany and his mother in Illinois of German parents. By the time

KLUNGEL'S LAGER
BEER SALOON,
BUILT AT
1623 N. WELLS
IN 1855.

Paddy became alderman in 1933, his ward was so ethnically mixed that there was no particular benefit in declaring himself to be Irish rather than German. Among the politicians of his time, however, the rule was when in doubt, be Irish.

The 43rd Ward was one of the most diverse in the city. On the east, it took in the Gold Coast, including the Ambassador Hotels and the Cardinal's mansion. Its southern border was a slum, which later became Cabrini Green. At its center was the old Cabbage Patch community, containing a German-language movie house, a few German restaurants, and numerous bars and businesses. The population was made up of Japanese, Finns, Hungarians, Italians, Irish, Syrians, Armenians, Swedes, and Poles. The physical appearance of the ward was as varied as its population. Parts looked like typical inner city areas; others were more like suburbs.

Paddy was the stereotype of a Chicago pol. He was huge (nearly 300 pounds), gregarious, and fiercely Democratic. From nine a.m. on, anyone wandering into the De Luxe would find Paddy sitting at a table with one of his executive assistants. (He was always there by nine in case someone had a brother who had been arrested or a relative who needed to be admitted to the hospital without a lot of red tape.) "You got to keep in touch," was his motto.

There were 40,000 votes in Paddy's ward monitored by 76 precinct captains, each holding a city, state, or county job. The Alderman admitted that he had some very nice jobs to give out—paying from $250 to $350 a month. All a fellow had to do was keep track of the votes in his precinct and get out the Democratic voters when it counted. Paddy demanded to know within one percentage point how the vote would turn out in any given precinct, and anyone who failed to keep track of the votes was unceremoniously ousted.

Like any successful politician, Paddy took care of his people. If there was a hole in a front sidewalk, a precinct captain would ring the doorbell about a week before an election and ask if the constituent was interested in having it fixed. There was never any doubt about what it would take to have the repair done.

Then, as now, getting voters out for local elections could be difficult, but Paddy had his methods. He would call in a precinct captain and ask how many voters he thought he could get to the polls. If the fellow answered with a low, but reasonable, figure, Paddy would hint that a better job and a little something extra for the kids might be found if the worker could manage at least 50 more votes. Usually, he got 150 more, and when he was sure of a victory on election night, he would have a party for the entire ward. In his signature silk top hat and frock coat, he would twirl his cane and dance around the De Luxe singing *Chicago, Chicago, That Toddlin' Town*.

While the Gold Coast was then part of the 43rd Ward, it was not Paddy's favorite neighborhood. People there didn't need his extra favors and couldn't be relied on to do the organization work. Paddy observed that many Gold Coast residents were Republicans and were always complaining about dirty streets and bad lighting, and not enough cops. "But when you come right down to it," he pointed out, "they only got one vote apiece, just like everybody else."

Bauler was a firm believer that one favor deserved another, and he had no patience with reformers. He called them political science kids, and declared Chicago ain't ready for reform. He saw his job in very simple terms—collect the garbage, repair the streets, clean the sidewalks and the people will vote for you. "People want service," he said, "not reform."

Paddy retired from the Council in 1967, the last of the saloon-keeping politicians. By the time he died in 1977, probably about 20 years too late according to journalist William Brashler, his cronies were all dead, or dying. His flamboyant style had gone out of date, and his 43rd Ward had become the domain of reformers.

CHAPTER SIX

YOU OUGHTA' BE IN PICTURES
Hollywood By The Lake

In the early 1900s, Chicago became, for a very brief period, the motion picture capital of the world, and Old Town was an important part of that fame. In 1907, Chicago had 116 nickelodeons, 10 vaudeville houses (which patrons could enter for ten cents), and 19 penny arcades showing early movies. At that time, there was no Hollywood, and most films were made on the East Coast. Businessman George K. Spoor, an early Crilly Court tenant, decided to bring filmmaking to the Midwest. He and cowboy actor G. M. (Bronco) Billy Anderson formed a partnership and built a studio at 1345 W. Argyle. They called it the Essanay (S & A) Film Company. Cross-eyed comedian Ben Turpin was Essanay's first star. Anderson stood behind the camera and filmed Turpin skating up and down Wells Street, bumping into bystanders. People who ran after him usually wound up in the feature as extras. Spoor staged the first Keystone Cops chase down Eugenie Street and through Crilly Court. Essanay also filmed the first Charlie Chaplin feature comedy, *His New Job,* in Old Town with screen legend Gloria Swanson and comedian Ben Turpin in small roles.

Chaplin's experience with Essanay was initally profitable for the company, but frustrating for the actor. He was actually signed by Anderson in California without Spoor's knowledge. Anderson promised the comedian $1,250 per week plus a $10,000 signing bonus. Spoor, who had never even heard of Chaplin, was furious at the terms. At that time, the top studio comics were making a weekly salary of $75. Though he agreed to honor the contract, he made it very difficult for Chaplin to get his signing bonus.

CHARLIE CHAPLIN GETS OFF THE TRAIN IN CHICAGO IN 1914 TO STAR IN HIS FIRST FEATURE COMEDY, *HIS NEW JOB*. MOVIE LEGEND GLORIA SWANSON HAD A BIT PART IN THE FILM.

Despite the financial haggling, Charlie was prepared to go to work. He rented a penthouse at 2800 N. Pine Grove, and went shopping on State Street, where he bought his signature baggy pants and oversized shoes. The Little Tramp was about to make his Chicago debut.

Spoor turned out dozens of 20-minute shorts for about $1,000 apiece. (Each film grossed more than $20,000.) He kept his film in an icebox and threw lavish parties for his stars, who included later movie idols Francis X. Bushman (for whom the famous Lincoln Park Zoo ape was named), Gloria Swanson, Wallace Beery, and, of course, Charlie Chaplin. These actors were paid about $15 per week ($20 if they worked on Saturdays). Chaplin's $1,250 per week salary did not endear him to his colleagues.

After the film was completed, Chaplin refused to work with Spoor again. He left Chicago and went to work in Essanay's California studio until 1916, when his contract was up. Then he signed with another studio. Chaplin's defection, along with other legal problems, was the beginning of the end for Essanay.

By 1918, the movie industry moved to Hollywood, and Essanay closed. While most of those connected with motion picture production went west, Spoor did not join the migration. He invested much of his personal fortune into a film process called natural vision. But the coming of sound in motion pictures and the lack of investment capital brought about by the Great Depression doomed the process. Down, but not out, Spoor invested the money he had left in Texas oilfields. This investment made him a rich man once again. He remained in Chicago until his death in 1953 at the age of 81.

AS TIME GOES BY

Going Down

Chicago and the north side enjoyed prosperity throughout the teens and into the early 1920s. Business was good, jobs were plentiful, and money was available. But the problems of the world at large: economic, political, and social infiltrated the Midwest and sent the area on a downward slide. After World War I, deterioration set in for two decades. The Great Depression brought hard times to the area, as it did almost everywhere. Even though a majority of the population did not invest in the stock market, the crash left its impact on society as a whole. One out of every four workers was unemployed, and Help Wanted signs in store windows were replaced by those reading No Help Wanted.

In many of the large, older homes, partitions were put up to create smaller and smaller rooms. Old Town was filled with flea-bag flophouses and transient hotels, many of which did not have indoor plumbing, central heating, or electricity. Families in two-and three-flat buildings huddled in front of the coal or wood burning stoves in their parlors to keep warm. Gardens were neglected and back yards collected rubbish. Even the five prestigious Louis Sullivan row houses on Lincoln Park West were turned into rooming houses accommodating as many as 25 families at a time. Street gangs infested the area surrounding St. Michael's Church, and bands of gypsies staked their claims on the low-rent tenements.

Two of the major automobile companies made news in 1930. Duesenberg came out with the Torpedo Phaeton touring car whose top folded into the rear deck, and Cadillac produced a roadster with the first auto safety glass. Neither of these innovations meant much to most Old Town residents who could not afford automobiles. For seven cents (three cents for children), they rode the Chicago Surface Line streetcars to work or to look for jobs. Children amused themselves by flipping the cars while in motion or hanging on the outside.

In this troubled time, many residents turned to the church for assistance and spiritual guidance. St. Michael's was filled with people who went to mass, vespers, benediction, and holy hour. The pastor was both spiritual leader and social worker, helping his parishioners get food, clothing, and jobs.

As Crilly Goes

Much of the history of Old Town in the early 20th century can be told through the rise, fall, and resurrection of Crilly Court. Crilly Court first belonged to Stephen F. Gale, Chicago's first stationer and first Fire Chief. In 1845, Gale owned 45 acres of farm and meadowland just north of the city limits. After he subdivided the property in 1845, it became part of the City of Chicago. Charles Canda, a Frenchman, bought the inside lots from Wells to Sedgwick and from Eugenie to St. Paul. He built a home with a barn and orchard and lived there until his death in 1854. After Canda died, his widow Adele took over the west half of the property and his brother Colonel Florimond Canda claimed the eastern section. (St. Paul Avenue was called Florimond Street until 1936.) Florimond had settled in Chicago in 1843, after having fought at the battle of Waterloo under Napoleon Bonaparte. In 1877, the Colonel sold his tract to south side contractor Daniel Crilly. Crilly Court was cut through the center of this property, and during the next few years, Mr. Crilly built houses and apartments as rental properties on either side of the street. Carved above the doorways of the apartment buildings on the east side of the street are the names of Mr. Crilly's children: Isabelle, Oliver, Erminnie, and Edgar. The building that fronts on Wells was later designated by the Chicago Landmarks Commission Guidelines as one of the city's twelve typical building types and cited as a model for store fronts with apartments above.

Carolyn Blackmon

THE CRILLY COURT HOUSES (AND APARTMENTS) WERE BUILT AS RENTAL PROPERTIES FOR PROFESSIONALS IN 1885 BY SOUTH SIDE DEVELOPER DANIEL CRILLY. THE APARTMENTS ON THE EAST SIDE OF THE STREET HAVE THE NAMES OF HIS CHILDREN CARVED ABOVE THE ENTRYWAYS.

Over the years, the Crilly estate rented to many well-known Chicagoans, including Cy de Vry, Director of the Lincoln Park Zoo, poet and newspaperman Eugene Field, George Spoor, the moviemaker, and Haddon Sundbloom, the creator of the man on the Quaker Oats box and Aunt Jemima. For more than 35 years, Sundbloom's Coca Cola Santa was an annual Christmas feature world-wide. A religion editor lived there between visits to his favorite nudist camp. Later residents included Alderman Paddy Bauler's grandchildren (Bauler was a frequent visitor), poet, Henry Rago, and a faded beauty from the Ziegfield Follies of 1907. At one time, an authority on ribbons, a pair of concert pianists, a political speech writer, a film editor, a literary columnist, a survivor of the Alaskan Gold Rush, and a neighborhood grocer all resided in the same row of buildings.

A Fight for Social Justice

The house at 1710 N. Crilly Court and one of its early tenants are now receiving national attention. Henry Gerber migrated to Chicago in 1913 from Germany and went to work at Montgomery Wards. With the outbreak of World War I, Gerber was interned as an enemy alien, along with many other German immigrants, and given the option of internment or military service. He chose military service. After the war, from 1920 to 1923, he served with the U.S. Army of Occupation in Germany at Coblenz. During this time, Gerber identified himself as homosexual and immersed himself in the large gay rights movement there. He subscribed to several gay periodicals and even contributed to some of them. He made a number of trips to Berlin and was in contact with leading gay organizations, including the Society for Human Rights, founded in 1919, and the Scientific Humanitarian Committee, the first-ever gay civil rights group.

Watercolor: A. Glen Resch; Photo: Norman Baugher

Gerber returned to Chicago and moved into the house at 1710 N. Crilly Court. He was immediately frustrated to find no gay rights organization in the United States. He determined to start one because of Chicago's large gay subculture. Since homosexuality was illegal, gay men and women had developed a clandestine existence of double lives, underground social clubs, and a system of dress and speech codes to recognize each other.

Gerber formed a group called the Society for

THE DISCREET CHARM OF CRILLY COURT BY A. GLEN RESCH EXHIBITOR IN THE OLD TOWN ART FAIR FOR MORE THAN FORTY YEARS. THE GERBER / BAUGHER HOUSE AT 1710 N. CRILLY COURT

Human Rights through which he hoped to educate the public about homosexuality and improve the plight of homosexuals in the United States. He appealed to his gay friends and to prominent individuals and medical authorities for support. He was, for the most part, unsuccessful in his efforts. He did manage to convince six individuals to become national officers of his organization, although they were mostly poor and illiterate— not the upstanding and influential persons he thought necessary for an effective organization. The group was granted a charter by the State of Illinois on December 10, 1924. As secretary of the society, Gerber's apartment served as the group's headquarters. Since 1710 was a rooming house, it is likely that Gerber rented a bedroom and used the basement for a meeting space. Gerber led meetings and produced the Society's newsletter.

When Gerber moved to Oak Street, his apartment was raided and he was arrested. Police confiscated his diaries, literature, and typewriter. After two trials, his case was dismissed because officers had conducted their raid and search without a warrant. Though the judge ordered that all his property be returned, he never retrieved his diaries or any materials pertaining to the Society. Gerber was dismissed from his job at the post office for conduct unbecoming a postal worker.

He then moved to New York City where he reenlisted in the army and served for 17 more years. In that computerless era, his record did not follow him, and there was no problem with his reenlistment. He died in a veteran's home in Washington, D.C. in 1972 at the age of 80.

Gerber's tenure on Crillly Court was significant because his room in the house at 1710 served as the founding headquarters of the nation's first gay civil rights movement, and the address appears on the State of Illinois charter as the Society's business address.

Until 1920, the Crilly houses were a rather stately group of Queen Anne style row homes occupied by business and professional people. By the late twenties they too had become seedy tenements whose landladies sat on their front stoops barefoot and tossed trash in their back yards. When Kappy and Alexander Maley rented the house at 1716 Crilly Court in 1937, they were appalled at its condition. Already small rooms had been chopped in half. Pay phones were found all over the house. The single bathroom was in such terrible condition that it had to be completely redone. The owner, Edgar Crilly, agreed to put in new carpeting and build a second bathroom. He also had the entire house painted. For this, the Maley's promised to pay $50 per month in rent.

GOING UP

After the Maleys moved in, the O'Tooles (she was Irma Koenigsberg, the tavern owner's daughter) purchased the house at 1706 N. Crilly Court for three thousand dollars and fixed it up inside and out, prompting the Maleys to further improve their place. The house at 1704 had such a well-maintained appearance that Kappy stopped by one day to get some decorating ideas. She was received by a handsome lady of a certain age and a beautiful younger one. Midway through the visit, she realized that she was consulting with the Madam and resident of a call house. It is not known exactly what decorating tips Mrs. Maley came away with. One week later, however, Mr. Maley was awakened at 3:00 a.m. by a loud knocking on the front door. When he opened the upstairs window, a cab driver asked if the Madam was in. Without thinking, Alexander Maley replied, "Yes, but she's in bed." A disappointed cabbie and his fares climbed back in their vehicle and drove away.

Within a very short period of time, other young couples purchased houses in the row: the Spencers at 1708, Isabel and John Drum at 1710, Virginia and Bob Leamington at 1712, and Barbara and Murray Washburne at 1720. Crilly Court was once again becoming a desirable place to live.

PADDY BAULER'S DE LUXE GARDENS AT THE SOUTHEAST CORNER OF SEDGWICK AND NORTH AVENUE. VARIETY OF WOOD, BRICK AND STONE BUILDINGS BUILT AFTER THE CHICAO FIRE.

The neighborhood even acquired a certain cultural caché (despite the fact that Schwerm's Drug Store at Sedgwick and Menomonee still sold leeches as cure-alls). Between 1938 and 1951, the great New Yorker essayist (and notorious Chicago basher) A. J. Liebling visited Chicago on numerous occasions to gather material for a series of articles he was writing for the magazine. The New Yorker later compiled these articles into a book called *Chicago, the Second City*. During one of his visits, he stayed with friends on Crilly Court, the Robert C. McNamaras, while doing research on the 43rd Ward and its colorful alderman, Mathias (Paddy) Bauler. McNamara's son, Norris, who currently lives on West Eugenie, recalls that Liebling turned out pages of acid commentary about Bauler and the 43rd Ward while sitting at their dining room table. It would seem that he was immune to the charms of both Crilly Court and the City of Chicago.

In 1949, Kay Bowers, who lived at 1708 and was a former music director of the Latin School, started giving lessons on the recorder for neighborhood children and their mothers in her basement. To show off their talents, they held lively concerts for sometimes reluctant fathers and friends. Thanks to the intervention of the Vice Squad, taxicabs stopped driving up at three in the morning inquiring after the Madam. By 1951, the cost of a house on Crilly Court had risen to a whopping $12,000.

Crilly Court was not the only street in Old Town experiencing an urban renaissance. In 1948, a group of homeowners started an association and began fixing up houses throughout the neighborhood. Artists Frank and Fern Dennison Hoffman bought a rowhouse on Wisconsin and remodeled it. Shortly thereafter, James Beverly, the head librarian for Judge John Gutnecht, and his wife Hildred, chief antiques buyer for Marshall Field & Company, bought next door to the Hoffmans and did extensive renovation. They sold that house and redid three row houses southeast of Wisconsin on Lincoln. With remodeling came cleanup of the grounds. Before long, most houses in the area had either gardens or window boxes, and a few had terraces on their garage roofs.

In 1950, this same group put on an art fair which brought the neighborhood to the attention of the broader metropolitan community. Some strollers liked the neighborhood so well, they decided to move in. In no time Victorian gingerbread embellishments were coming down and houses were doing double duty as residences and studios.

CHAPTER NINE

ICHi-26862 Photographer: Tom H. Long

A GRAND BURG
SAYS SANDBURG
A Place of Substantial Renown

S T. LOUIS *has Gaslight Square*
New York has Greenwich Village
New Orleans has The French Quarter
Paris has Montmartre
Chicago has Old Town.

Rehab fever spread to the business community, and enterprising owners
undertook significant changes to their facades. While the Space Age
focused the rest of the nation on the future, the new look of Old Town in
the 50s and early 60s was achieved by looking back. Antique shops sprang
up overnight. Buildings underwent reverse face lifting as merchants tried
to make their establishments look old. Vintage saloons, ice cream parlors,
penny candy vending carts, Victorian emporiums, and Depression-style
soup kitchens dotted Wells Street in what was dubbed the new beau style.
Once again, Chicago descended on Old Town, this time on Gray Line
buses.

The area was being compared to Greenwich Village, albeit a little less crowded and touristy. The Old Town shopping area took pride in its smallness and offered shoppers an alternative to department stores. Old Town had 174 businesses, mostly shops. The shops rented for about $250 per month; the restaurants for thousands. House sales rose by 25 percent, and it was easy to get business and mortgage money.

At the Earl of Old Town, folk music poured from the throats and guitars of musicians Steve Goodman and John Prine. On any Saturday night, Goodman, who left us far too soon, would answer the inevitable request for The City of New Orleans, and Prine for his bittersweet ballad, The Old Folks.

Piper's Alley became the in place to go, along with numerous trendy restaurants and boutiques south of North Avenue: The Pickle Barrel, Chances Are, Paul Bunyon's, Bizarre Bazaar, Bourbon Street, Big John's, the Plugged Nickel, Mother Blues, and the Fudge Pot (still doing business). Piper's Bakery was reincarnated as a restaurant (That Steak Joynt) and a warren of little shops, eateries, and watering holes. Those who walked inside the Alley found poster shops featuring the latest poses of the Beatles and Bob Dylan, candle makers, arts and crafts studios, bookstores, and earrings, earrings, earrings.

Top jazzmen played at the Plugged Nickel and Mother Blues. At Chances R, patrons cluttered the floor with peanut shells and filled the air with raucous chatter. From Monday through Saturday, the crowds started pouring in at noon. By 8:00 p.m., the merriment was in full swing. On weekends, it was SRO—noisy, congested, and great fun.

So many people came in from the suburbs that *Tourist Go Home* signs actually appeared in windows of the residents' favorite hangouts. At the Old Town Ale House on North Avenue, about 80 regulars got so fed

Inset: ICHi-26328 Photographer, Walter Krutz; large photo: ICHi-24998 Photographer, Henry Reichel

INSET ABOVE: PIPER'S ALLLEY, 1602-1610 N. WELLS STREET, 1965. MRS. PIPER'S BAKERY IS TO THE LEFT OF THE TIFFANY-STYLE ENTRY.

PIPER'S ALLEY, 1964, BEFORE THE ENTRY WAS ENCLOSED. THE INTERIOR COURT WAS HOME TO SHOPS AND RESTAURANTS

up with the influx of outsiders that they chartered a bus one Sunday morning to take them to the suburbs. The sign on the bus read Old Town Strikes Back. They descended upon the lawn of a Mrs. Callahan in Lincolnwood about 11:00 a.m. and asked for beer. Having none, the best Mrs. Callahan could do was offer the use of her washroom, for which some riders queued up. Others spread out over the neighborhood making the same request. Of course, there was a newspaperman conveniently on hand to photograph the bizarre event. And what was the effect of this pilgrimage? The next weekend there were more suburbanites than ever in Old Town, including Mrs. Callahan.

Second City

No description of Old Town at mid-twentieth century would be complete without mentioning its most famous group of entertainers, The Second City Players. On December 16, 1959, Beethoven's 189th birthday, Second City opened in a converted Chinese laundry on North Wells Street. Cast members stepped onstage and were greeted by the applause of more than 200 opening night patrons who couldn't stop laughing. Despite the fears of

The Second City

TOP LEFT: SECOND CITY, 1616 N. WELLS STREET. EXTERIOR DETAIL ORIGINALLY FROM THE SCHILLER BUILDING.

TOP RIGHT: THE CAST OF SECOND CITY, 1960. LEFT TO RIGHT, EUGENE TROBNIK, BARBARA HARRIS, ALAN ARKIN, PAUL SAND, BILL MATHIEU, MINA KOLB, SEVERN DARDEN, ANDREW DUNCAN.

LEFT: THE SECOND CITY CAST, 1974. LEFT TO RIGHT, JOHN CANDY, DAN AKROYD, EUGENE LEVY, ROSEMARY RADELIFFE, AND GILDA RADNER.

some actors that it might be a one-night stand, the audience kept coming.

The group, which included Mike Nichols, Elaine May, and Paul Sills, had gotten together in 1953 at the University of Chicago. Within a few years, they moved to the north side and started playing the clubs there. They had originally planned to have a coffee shop where they would just sit around and entertain. That evolved into a cabaret-like theater revue with set themes. When this idea didn't click, Mike Nichols, who had gone on to Broadway, suggested they drop the theme idea and just do scenes. Within a few months, The Second City Players were selling out every performance. They even expanded to other cities and to Canada, and they are still going strong. Their alums include actor/director Harold Ramis, Bonnie Hunt, Peter Boyle, Alan Arkin, Joan Rivers, Barbara Harris, Bill

Murray, Dan Ackroyd, Mike Myers, and late greats John Belushi, Gilda Radner, John Candy, and Chris Farley.

Roller Coaster Ride

From 1961 to 1963, forty-five new businesses were established on Wells Street from Division to Second City. There were also six on Sedgwick and three on Larrabee. Property values skyrocketed, and developers were buying everything they could get their hands on. Prosperity reigned. And then, it ended. The free-spending tourists were gone; and Old Town was infiltrated by young people who looked, but did not buy. The saloons began to close, shops were vacated, and cafés and lounges became adult bookstores. Despite decreasing revenues, however, rents remained high, discouraging many would-be entrepreneurs.

But Old Town was not to be relegated to the porn scrap heap. In the mid-1970s, well-known entertainers returned, bringing their acts to clubs like Zanies and Second City. Developers bought and restored more old greystone buildings and three-flats. Walgreens, Treasure Island, and the North Federal Savings Bank moved in. Later, Starbucks, dry cleaners, and galleries took over store fronts formerly frequented by head shops.

Urban renewal allowed young professionals to purchase some of the great old houses in Old Town, but rehab was not always easy. Buyers experienced the usual problems of tradesmen who made promises they failed to keep. In addition, many contractors were not interested in doing work for an owner seeking an urban renewal loan. A two-month job often took six months or more to complete because the owners were waiting for a loan to come through. Middle and upper middle class couples discovered that their chic little area was not so chic when they had to wash lettuce in the bath tub because of a stalled kitchen rehab.

By 1977, the federal government and private investors had poured more than $270 million into development projects. Both commercial Wells Street and the noncommercial neighborhood had gone upscale. Range Rovers became the cars of choice for young mothers dropping their kids off at elementary school or the Menomonee Club.

STREETCAR AT EUGENIE & WELLS, 1940S.

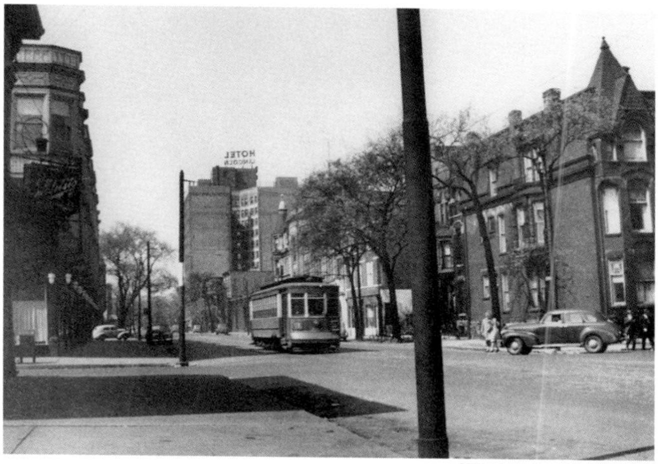

OTTA 98013

CHAPTER TEN

CHICAGO
A Wonderful City For Opportunity

What Do You Do For a Living?

Occupations in Old Town changed with changing times. The farmers and trades-people of the nineteenth century gave way to a group of artistic types in the late 1930s. Musicians, artists, writers, theater performers, radio, and film people were drawn to the neighborhood bringing, once again, a wonderful diversity. By 1950, when North Town was officially designated Old Town, its more than 8,000 residents included such entertainment and cultural icons as historian Paul Angle, artist Edgar Miller, Pulitzer Prize winning cartoonist Bill Mauldin, television's Don Herbert (Mr. Wizard), writer Herman Kogan, and painter Francis Chapin.

These artists exercised their creativity in Old Town through the late '70s, and then they began to drift away. Still, Old Town remained a heterogeneous and caring community. Neighbor and professional photog-

JUHL'S FANCY
GROCERIES, 225 W.
MENOMONEE, 1950.

WE GATHER
TOGETHER.
ST. JAMES CHURCH,
1700 BLOCK OF
NORTH PARK, 1960S.

ICHi-26300 Photographer, Betty Henderson

OTTA 98024

rapher Rona Talcott called it a small town with a twist. ABC TV editor
Carol Cross described it as a family of neighbors who look out for each
other.

In the '90s people who made their living in the financial world,
especially traders and bankers, moved in, attracted by the close-in location
and ambiance of the neighborhood, along with a large group of technolo-
gy experts. This richly diverse professional group characterizes the
Triangle in the early part of the 21st century.

ONE OF TWO OLD TOWN TRIANGLE HISTORIC
DISTRICT MARKERS AT MENOMONEE & WELLS
STREETS—CHICAGO LANDMARKS COMMISSION
PLAQUE.

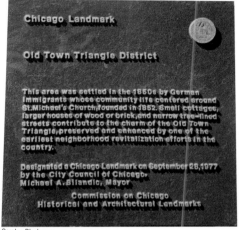

Carolyn Blackmon

CHAPTER ELEVEN

NOW WE BELONG TO THE AGES

Workman, Spare That House

At the height of the urban renewal period in the '70s, more than 600 residential units were leveled between North Halsted, Lincoln, and Webster and replaced with high-priced town houses. As churches, schools, and factories were converted to houses, a real battle began to control density. Developers who thought they could build high rises on every vacant lot in the area reckoned without some stalwart preservationists from the Old Town Triangle Association; and they certainly reckoned without Amy Forkert.

Once in Love with Amy

Amy Forkert, who has often been called the First Lady of Old Town, has lived at 1836 N. Lincoln Park West since 1951. She is a member of the National Trust for Historic Preservation and the Society of Architectural Historians. When her Old Town was in danger of going the way of other

TOP: INSTALLATION OF THE OLD TOWN TRIANGLE HISTORIC DISTRICT PLAQUE, 1987. LEFT TO RIGHT EDWIN EISENDRATH, 43RD WARD ALDERMAN, DIANE GONZALEZ, COMMITTEE MEMBER, MRS. O. M. FORKERT, HISTORIC DISTRICT NOMINATING COMMITTEE, BRUNO AST, PRESIDENT, OLD TOWN TRIANGLE ASSOCIATION.

INSET: SECOND OF TWO OLD TOWN TRIANGLE HISTORIC DISTRICT MARKERS AT MENOMONEE & WELLS STREETS— UNITED STATES DEPARTMENT OF INTERIOR PLAQUE.

THE OLD TOWN TRIANGLE HISTORIC DISTRICT HAS BEEN PLACED ON THE NATIONAL REGISTER OF HISTORIC PLACES BY THE UNITED STATES DEPARTMENT OF THE INTERIOR NOVEMBER 11, 1984

Carolyn Blackmon

city neighborhoods that were tearing down architecturally significant structures to put up high-rise apartment buildings and contemporary monstrosities, she marshaled her forces. For the next ten years, from 1967 to 1977, she gathered documentation showing the worth of the neighborhood. She learned everything possible about the 523 structures in the Triangle, soliciting information from the Cook County Recorder of Deeds, the City Department of Sewers, and from neighbors. She organized block meetings to gather and consolidate information and supervised distribution of questionnaires from the Chicago Historical and Architectural Landmarks organization to Triangle residents.

Amy and her committee compiled it all, noting the year each structure was built, its architect, the first owners, the condition of the exteriors, including building materials, architectural styles, building use, and interesting anecdotal information. When all the stories had been recorded, the documentation collected, and the memories recollected, Leigh Sills categorized, tabulated, and summarized the data. William G. Hyer, a retired advertising executive, then wrote the narrative and descriptive material. He recorded that the average residential density was 17.4 structures per acre, with a concentration of small houses on small lots with narrow setbacks. He described a mix of three- and four-story brick flats, scattered among brick, brick and frame, and frame cottages. The Old Town Triangle Historic District, he wrote, contains an early urban working-class fabric. Of the 523 structures encompassed by the Old Town Triangle Historic District, 198 have been evaluated as significant architecturally, significant historically, or both. When rear dwellings of the significant structures are included, the total rises to 213. About 225 structures have been identified as contributing to the character of the District. These structures contain 32 rear dwellings, which brings the total to 256. Nineteen of the non-contributing structures built before 1930 have been so classified because of the structure being architecturally altered to a point where they are difficult to restore. Thirty-five are identified as non-contributing because they are new construction built after 1960. The non-contributing category also includes those structures considered intrusive. It appears that there was no new construction between 1928 and 1961. Rather, imaginative new restoration was undertaken in this period.

The Committee then presented the completed document to the Landmarks Commission. The Old Town Triangle District was designated a Chicago Landmark by the City Council of Chicago on September 28, 1977.

What a group they were, these preservationists who said NIMBY to developers and merchants seeking to fill empty lots with high-density buildings! What determination and courage they had to advise would-be buyers seeking to demolish small cottages and aging houses for big and different to go where big and different were more appropriate. But they prevailed, and for this, the neighborhood will be forever grateful.

You're a Little Rearranged, but You Really Haven't Changed: Old Town Architecture

[In the 1920s and '30s, other Chicago neighborhoods began replacing older, single-family houses with large apartment buildings. North Town chose to keep much of its original housing, as well as its character and charm. What new construction was undertaken consisted mainly of garages with servants' quarters above for chauffeurs of wealthy Gold Coast homeowners such as John G. Shedd (Chairman of Marshall Field & Co), Phillip and Watson Armour, Frederik Rawson (President of the Union

1838 LINCOLN PARK WEST, KNOWN AS ONE OF THE WACKER HOUSES. BUILT IN 1874, IT HAS THE CHARACTERISTICS OF A SWISS CHALET.

Trust Co.), Alfred Cowles (Chairman of Rialto Trust), Edward Furst (Head of the Miehle Printing Co.), and John Harding (restaurateur). Today, most of these garages have been converted to family residences.]

One does not have to imagine how the Old Town neighborhood looked one hundred years ago. Walking its streets brings a stroller face-to-face with history. Writing about Old Town architecture a few years ago, noted Chicago architect, Seymour Goldstein observed: "Historically speaking, Old Town is a conglomeration of what might be termed the anonymous-builder's architecture—men in the building trades of yesterday who were often more adept and conscientious than some professional architects." Goldstein noted that, in the late 1800s and early 1900s masons were the real architects in Old Town. Contractors employed a large number of Italian masons and stonecutters to do new building construction, as is evidenced by the roof structures and the top corbelling.

"The elegance of the neighborhood defies time. The houses are more worthwhile now, for some of the valid patterns of living, than many works of architecture that have been executed by some of the benighted architects of the latter 1800's. In Old Town," Goldstein continues, "you can see buildings executed by humble and honest men who have achieved something sincere. In many instances overly sentimental, perhaps. But, nonetheless, their genuine naivete gave a scale that seems human, not the lifeless expression of a machined art. Certainly in this human scale, we can find a raison d'etre for Old Town's current popularity and a heartening message for our own day."

These are a few of the buildings created by those "benighted architects of the latter 1800's" that still grace the streets of our neighborhood.

THE OLSEN-HANSEN ROW HOUSES in the 100 block of West Eugenie. These houses were designed by Norwegian-born architect Harald Hansen, who later headed the Department of Architecture at the University of Illinois. Hansen bought the property from Adolph Olsen in 1886. Originally, there were 12 houses, nine on Eugenie and three around the corner on Wells. Only the five houses closest to Wells remain standing, among them, the architect's own residence. At one time, the block was called Pill Row since many of its residents were doctors. The facades of these Queen Anne structures, together with their irregular rooflines and combinations of materials, are typical of Victorian design.

THE JOHN BOLAND RESIDENCE at 221 W. Eugenie was built in 1884. Notable features of the building are segmentally arched windows and a projecting bay crowned with a terra cotta pediment. Boland, a plasterer, was in charge of the plasterwork projects for the Shedd Aquarium, the Adler Planetarium, the Mexican Opera House, and the Palace of Justice in Guatemala. He was also involved in the plasterwork for the Columbian Exposition in 1893.

THE PHILIP HENRICI HOUSE. Henrici was a prominent Chicago restaurateur. His Romanesque home at Lincoln Avenue and Wisconsin Streets has a cast iron balustrade at the roof and a roughly textured frieze of carved stone. At one time, there were horse stables in the rear of the residence.

THE WACKER HOUSE. In 1874, real estate developer, Frederick Wacker commissioned a baroque structure at 1838 Lincoln Park West (then called Franklin Street). The original house was built just before new regulations prohibited wood construction in that part of the city destroyed by the fire. The form is typical of a Chicago cottage, but the wide overhanging veranda supported by curved wooden brackets, openwork hoods above the windows, and carved wooden spindle railings flanking a broad stairway make the house look like a Swiss chalet.

1836 LINCOLN PARK WEST, ANOTHER WACKER HOUSE, BUILT IN 1884. THE HOUSE IS ARCHITECTURALLY SIGNIFICANT FOR ITS FLORAL MOTIF AND METAL FILAGREE RAILING.

CHARLES WACKER, built a more modest home at 1836 Lincoln Park West. This house was distinctive for its small eave brackets, intricate turned columns, and wood fretwork for the entrance canopy. Charles Wacker became one of Chicago's most prominent citizens. He was the youngest director of the 1893 World's Columbian Exposition, a very successful brewer, a building association member, and Chairman of the Chicago Plan Commission for 17 years. Wacker Drive was later named for him. When he married, he gave the smaller house at 1836 to his mother-in-law. He and his wife moved into the large residence at 1838.

THE LOUIS SULLIVAN ROW HOUSES. Louis Sullivan, one of Chicago's most noted architects, was commissioned by Miss Ann Halsted in 1884 to build four row houses from 1826 to 1834 Lincoln Park West. Built as rental property, the houses are among the few surviving examples of early Sullivan design. He used the simplified Queen Anne style and his trademark terra-cotta ornamentation. These houses are among Old Town's architecturally significant treasures.

THE EISENDRATH HOUSES. The distinctive townhouses at 1842, 44, and 46 Lincoln Park West were built in 1873 for Nathan Eisendrath, a prosperous brickmaker. Their distinctive French influence is shown in the carved hoods over the windows and split-faced stone keystones. Architectural design students still study these features.

LEFT: CRILLY
TOWNHOUSES
ON THE WEST
SIDE OF N.
CRILLY COURT.

ICHi-23110, Kaufmann Fabry, 1940

LEFT: SULLIVAN
ROW HOUSES,
1826-34 LINCOLN
PARK WEST.
FIVE BRICK
ROWHOUSES,
BUILT BY FAMED
LOUIS SULLIVAN
IN 1884. THEY ARE
AMONG A FEW
SURVIVING
EXAMPLES OF
SULLIVAN'S EARLY
DESIGN. THE
HOUSES ARE
SIGNIFICANT FOR
THE TYPICAL
SULLIVAN TERRA-
COTTA
ORNAMENTATION.

Carolyn Blackmon

CRILLY COURT. In 1877, Daniel J. Crilly, a south side contractor, bought a large tract of land bounded by Wells Street, North Park, Eugenie, and St. Paul. He cut a one-block north-south street through the middle of the property and called it Crilly Court. On the east side of the street, he built four apartment houses with the names of each of his children carved above the doorways: Isabelle, Oliver, Erminnie, and Edgar. On the other side, Crilly constructed a group of simplified Queen Anne style row houses. A number of celebrities lived in the Crilly complex in the early days, including poet Eugene Field, who wrote his famous poem Little Boy Blue during his tenure.

THE TONK OR ANGEL DOOR HOUSE. In 1874, a French Renaissance house, later known as the Angel Door House, was built by Johann Tonk at 1817 N. Lincoln Park West. He first built a frame cottage on the back part of his lot. Later, using $60 of free building materials offered by the Aid Society after the Fire, he built the main house under the direction of a French architect. Mr. Tonk's son Max carved

THE HISTORY OF A NEIGHBORHOOD 51

LEFT : 1817 LINCOLN PARK WEST. FRENCH RENAISSANCE DESIGN, BUILT IN 1874. THE HOUSE IS KNOWN AS THE TONK OR ANGEL DOOR HOUSE.

RIGHT: 331 W. MENOMONEE

the Angel Doors. In 1881, the Tonks sold the home to a young grain broker, Erich Gerstenberg and his new bride. The Gerstenbergs converted the laundry wing of the house into a ballroom, which was the scene of many grand parties.

325-348 W. MENOMONEE STREET. These nine cottages give a good idea of how the community looked before the Fire. The tiny cottage at 348, on the edge of the alley, is a rare surviving example of a fire relief cottage. Immediately after the

Fire, the Relief & Aid Society supported the construction of these one-room houses, which could be moved by wagon to a burned-out lot. This one has been slightly enlarged and has new siding.

1763 N. NORTH PARK. The current home of the Old Town Triangle Association was a later addition to the neighborhood. It was built in 1922 by Graham, Anderson, Probst, & White as a garage with apartments above for chauffeurs of Gold Coast residents whose lots were too narrow to accommodate their cars. The garage space of the building was later remodeled to be used as meeting rooms and classrooms. The Old Town Triangle Association moved into the space in 1983.

OTTA archives: 98025

HOME OF THE OLD TOWN TRIANGLE ASSOCIATION, THE OLD TOWN ART CENTER, THE OLD TOWN GALLERY, FORUM FOR COMMUNITY MEETINGS, POLLING PLACE, ACTIVITY CENTER FOR CHILDREN, 1991 PHOTO

*T*HERE ARE FIVE THINGS *that are necessary to keep a community viable through the years: an understanding of residents' needs, a willingness to provide services responsive to those needs, an organization through which those services are delivered on an ongoing basis, open lines of communication between organization leaders and members, and a commitment to volunteerism among residents. The Old Town Triangle has addressed each of these elements.*

CHAPTER TWELVE

STAYING ALIVE
The Old Town Triangle Association

THE NEIGHBORHOOD IMPROVEMENTS COMMITTEE OVERSEES
PLANTING AND MAINTAINING TREES AND PARKWAYS

The Old Town Triangle is unique among the nation's urban neighborhoods. While more than one hundred years have passed since the first German farmers and masons planted cabbages and built simple cottages on this little section of Chicago's north side, the community is as vibrant and energetic today as it was then. It is not uncommon for city residents to know who lives next door or down any given block. It is rare that they know and inter-mingle with an entire community. Rarer still that they band together to share concerns, protect their neighborhood's architectural integrity, improve its open spaces, contribute to its cultural life, and insure efficient delivery of city services.

That the Triangle neighborhood does these things is due to the diligence and determination of the Old Town Triangle Association (OTTA) a nonprofit organization of residents established in 1948. (Appendix A page 135) This organization provides a forum for identifying and addressing matters that affect the well being of its members, maintaining property values, assuring that city services are kept up to standard, and building confidence in the commu-

Carolyn Blackmon

nity. Its method is organized self-help through cooperation among neighbors and neighborhood groups, citywide organizations, and city government. It also provides assistance to organizations and groups whose goals reflect the stated mission of the Association. The OTTA is guided by an eleven-member Board of Directors that meets monthly to consider neighborhood issues.

Getting the Job Done

A number of committees operate under the aegis of the Board of Directors to address local needs. These include the Historic District/Planning & Zoning Committee, the Neighborhood Improvements Committee, and the CAPS program.

Nearly thirty years ago, members of the Historic District Committee, which included neighbors Amy and Maurice Forkert, Bill Hyer, Mary Gehr, Paul and Darlene Fahrenkrog, and Leigh Sills succeeded in having most of the Old Town Triangle area designated as an Historic District by the Chicago City Council. Today, the Committee acts as a liaison between the Old Town community and the Landmarks Commission, reporting the Committee's recommendations and responding to questions of the commissioners.

Each month, members consider requests for proposed exterior changes to existing buildings, new construction, and requests for zoning changes in the Triangle. Their deliberations range from the appropriateness of building materials used in rehabbing and construction projects to the height of fences and building additions. The Guidelines for Alterations to Historic Buildings and New Construction, prepared by the Commission on Chicago Landmarks, serves as the basis for their recommendations. These recommendations are sent to the Alderman of the 43rd ward and to appropriate city commissions and departments for final approval.

Since neighborhood relations figure prominently in any rehab project, members of the Historic District/Planning & Zoning Committee work with neighbors to maintain good relations between persons who are making changes to their properties and those who live in adjoining houses.

The Neighborhood Improvements Committee oversees planting and maintaining trees and parkways in the Triangle and develops projects to enhance the quality of life for residents. They also supervise an annual

Carolyn Blackmon

clean-up day each spring which involves the efforts of many neighbors.

CAPS (Chicago Alternative Policing Strategy) is sponsored jointly by the Triangle and the Chicago Police Department to enhance neighborhood safety. Under CAPS, each of the City's 25 police districts is divided into beats, small geographic areas in which the Chicago Police Department, City agencies, and citizens work together to fight crime. A team of police officers is assigned to a beat for at least one year. This allows neighborhood residents and officers to get to know each other. Beat officers patrol the neighborhood, responding to police emergencies and working with citizens to identify and solve crime problems in the community. The Old Town Triangle is in the 18th District, Beat 1814.

Beat officers are supported by other police teams in the district who respond to emergency calls and focus on specific problems, such as gangs, drugs, and crimes against people. Other City agencies take care of conditions that can lead to crime, e.g., graffiti, abandoned buildings and cars, and broken streetlights.

Spreading the Word

The Triangle Association publishes a neighborhood newsletter, the *Old Town Times,* that keeps residents informed about relevant city and local events. It also provides information about Triangle-sponsored art classes;

meetings between the 18th District beat police and the neighbors; yoga classes; activities for children offered by the Menomonee Club; social get-togethers; and issue-oriented forums. Membership in the Association is maintained through the ongoing efforts of a Membership Committee.

Community Service

The Old Town Triangle Association addresses the interests of young people in the community through its sponsorship of Boy Scout Troop 79, a group of 35 young men who range in age from 11 to 17. The troop meets weekly to participate in activities that encourage character development, good citizenship, and mental and physical fitness. Cub Scout and Girl Scout programs are offered through the Menomonee Club for Boys and Girls.

The Menomonee Club for Boys and Girls was founded in 1946 by Triangle residents as a youth recreation center for children from six to sixteen years of age. In those early days, the Board of the Menomonee Club and the Board of the Old Town

NORTH END BOWLING CLUB, BUILT IN 1891. THE BUILDING, AT THE CORNER OF WILLOW AND NORTH PARK, WAS THE HOME OF THE MENOMONEE BOYS CLUB IN THE 1940S.

NEIGHBORHOOD BOYS SELLING PLANTS FOR THE MENOMONEE BOYS AND GIRLS CLUB IN FRONT OF THE ECONOMY STORE AT EUGENIE AND WELLS, 1950S.

Triangle Association consisted of the same officers and directors. As the activities and membership of the Menomonee Club veered beyond the confines of the Old Town Triangle and the Triangle Association became more involved in addressing the artistic, neighborhood improvement, and safety needs of its residents, the two became separate entities, though they remained committed to the goal of community service.

From its inception, the Menomonee Club offered a diverse program of activities that met the needs of the Triangle's young people, instructed them in skills that would improve both their minds and bodies, and taught them democratic values and citizenship within a framework of group activity. Parents and interested residents were invited to participate in the club's activities along with the students. The original membership fee was 50 cents (25 cents for those under twelve). In 1952, the club listed 133 registered members, but there were always more boys and girls using the club than there were paid members.

No longer exclusively a neighborhood meeting place, the Menomonee Club now provides activities for more than 1,500 children from junior kindergarten through the ninth grade representing over 50 schools. These activities include baseball, softball, basketball, soccer, kayaking and canoeing, judo, creative drama, magic, jazz & hip hop, photography, and various dance categories. The 50-cent membership fee is a memory, but the cost for participation in the club's many activities is still nominal and scholarships are available. The current Menomonee Board is made up of 28 officers and directors, mainly from the city's north side.

CHAPTER

THIRTEEN

EVERYTHING PASSES, ART IS ETERNAL

Norman Baugher

The Old Town Art Center

More than 40 years ago, Triangle founders affirmed their interest in the arts by establishing an art school to provide a friendly, low-key, learning environment for professional and non-professional artists. Instructors recruited from Chicago's artistic community currently offer classes in figure drawing, charcoal and pastel drawing, oil painting, and watercolor. Students in the Art Center present an annual exhibit of their works in the Old Town Art Gallery during the month of June. The classes are offered for a nominal fee to all interested adults, regardless of their experience or level of expertise.

AN ART CLASS AT THE OLD TOWN ART CENTER,
1763 N. NORTH PARK, JAMES WISNOWSKI, INSTRUCTOR. 2000

Leslie Wolfe

Another Opening, Another Show:
the Old Town Art Gallery

OTTA is sensitive to the plight of young artists who want to gain a following for their work but who often have difficulty securing space in the City's commercial galleries. In 1956, the Association established the Old Town Art Gallery. Chicago-area artists are invited to exhibit their works in a month-long show. The exhibits feature a variety of styles and media, including oil, watercolor, pastel, charcoal, quilt art, silk-screening, and sculpture. Viewers are able to purchase most pieces on exhibit.

POSTCARD FOR JUNE 2001 STUDENT ART OPENING AT THE OLD TOWN ART GALLERY. PAINTING BY ROSIE MACLEAN.

Phil Renaud

OTTA 98001 Photographer, Arnie Matanky

VIEW OF THE 1982 OLD TOWN ART FAIR FROM LINCOLN PARK PLACE ON 1920 N. CLARK STREET SHOWING THE INTERSECTION OF LINCOLN, LINCOLN PARK WEST, AND WISCONSIN.

Hi! Ho! Come to the Fair

The Old Town Art Fair, the oldest juried outdoor art fair in the nation, is the OTTA's most important activity and its chief means of support. The first fair, held in 1950, was called The Old Town Holiday. Anyone could enter, and participants displayed their art on fences and tables on Lincoln Park West and its two adjacent alleys. Seventy exhibitors showed everything from crocheted potholders to high quality oils and watercolors.

Old Town Holiday was, in reality, a big neighborhood party. Artists were both hosts and volunteer workers. Neighbors, friends, and a few outsiders made up the guest list, (which increased with each fair). There were no entry restrictions, and the definition of art was stretched to its outer limits. Not only was the event great fun, it was a smashing success—so much so that there was another fair the next year—and the next—and the next. The descriptor Outdoor Arts and Crafts Fair was added to the name Old Town Holiday in 1954, indicating the fair's evolution from a neighborhood party to a metropolitan event, though it was not officially designated The Old Town Art Fair until 1963.

As the fair grew in size and prestige, the selection process became more sophisticated. Entries came under the scrutiny of a jury of professional artists which enhanced the quality of work exhibited at the fair, and brought about many of its current features, including: a balanced offering of sculpture, painting, ceramics, jewelry-making, leather working, and other art media and the practice of having each artist donate a representative piece of work to the auction as his or her entry fee. The auction proceeds accrue to the Triangle Association and are a primary source of income for the fair.

Art Fair Chairs have also brought about a number of significant changes: Roger Skolnik (1988-89) initiated uniform booth sizes, eliminating the need for double rows of exhibitors on Lincoln Park West and Orleans Streets. Beverly Adilman (1990-91), Pat French (1992-93) and Justine Price (1994-95) started an Artists' Ambassadors Program and traveled to galleries, studios, and other shows nationwide to recruit artists for the Old Town Art Fair. Norman Baugher (1998-99) and Carolyn Blackmon(2000-2001) collaborated to refine the Committee structure and make running the fair more manageable and efficient.

Currently, more than 250 artists from the United States, Canada, and Europe participate. Some exhibitors are second generation: Jeffrey Gelick exhibited in 1999 with his wife Joyce. His mother, Ethel Gelick, exhibited between 1963 and 1983.

Where Does the Money Go?

While more than 50,000 patrons visit the Old Town Art Fair every year, most do not know how their donations are used. They might be both surprised and pleased to learn that they are supporting programs to improve conditions of life, work, recreation, health, education, and safety in one of Chicago's oldest and most treasured neighborhoods.

Triangle residents share two passions: a dedication to the arts and a commitment to neighborhood preservation. The Old Town Triangle Association uses a portion of its art fair proceeds each year to promote art study and appreciation through the operation of a neighborhood art center and gallery. The Art Center provides a friendly, low-key learning environment for both professional and non-professional artists seeking to fulfill their creative urges. The Triangle Art Gallery displays the works of local artists and holds a formal opening on the second Sunday of each month to which the public is invited.

To address its second commitment, the Old Town Triangle Association uses revenues from the art fair to implement neighborhood improvement and beautification programs: buying, planting, and maintaining trees, repairing parkways, and caring for small parks within the area.

Art Fair monies are also used to enhance civic activities through sponsorship of Boy Scout Troop 79 and the YMCA summer camp program for urban children. Currently, OTTA reinforces its commitment to educational excellence through support of the artist-in-residence program at LaSalle Elementary School, a computer software replacement program at Lincoln Elementary School, and an after-school computer training program in the Lincoln Park High School .

Despite the fair's phenomenal growth, it is still a volunteer effort requiring the participation of at least 800 volunteers, a General Chair and various sub-committee chairs. Volunteer committees include: Exhibitors, Grounds, Print Services, Community Relations, Advertising & Contributions, Art Fair Store, and Thank You Party.

It has often been said that artists are the heart of the fair, and the volunteers are its soul.

Who's Who — Then and Now

No history of the Old Town Triangle Association would be complete without mentioning a few of its movers and shakers. This list is by no means complete; it is merely representative of the hundreds of neighbors who have dedicated their time and talents to the founding and ongoing success of this organization.

JAMES E. BEVERLY was the first Triangle President from 1948 to 1950. According to Mr. Beverly: the Civilian Defense Organization of World War II was the forerunner of the Old Town Triangle Association, explaining that block defense and victory garden clubs gave residents opportunities to meet and do things with their neighbors to a degree never before possible in a busy metropolitan community. The present boundaries of the Triangle were set at that time as a unit of the Greater Chicago Defense System. Beverly chaired the first town meeting in 1948 and came up with a seven-point program of objectives. He was instrumental in getting the Chicago Plan Commission to designate the community a conservation area.

ROBERT M. SWITZER succeeded Beverly. He won first prize in the Fifth Annual Old Town Holiday (Art Fair) for his beautiful enclosed patio at 1846 N. Orleans. Coming in second in that category was D.F. Crilly who took the honors for the large Crilly Court patio.

JOE VITALE, Executive Director of the North Town Boys Club in 1945 was instrumental in renting space, securing staff, and organizing activities that made up the program of the Menomonee Club. These activities were at first reserved for boys but later expanded to include neighborhood girls. Mr. Vitale still resides in the 1800 block of North Orleans.

FRANCIS CHAPIN. There are not enough accolades to describe the contributions of this talented man. He was a superb artist, a lecturer, a good neighbor, and a friend to Old Town. Despite his worldwide recognition, he continued to exhibit his works at the Old Town Art Fair and the Old Town Triangle Center. He gave generously of his time to the neighborhood and acted as a consultant to the Triangle Association on numerous occasions.

PAUL ANGLE, a renowned Lincoln scholar, Director of the Chicago Historical Society, and noted journalist, lived in the Triangle for nearly 30 years. Mr. Angle, his wife, and his daughter, Paula, never tired of working for and writing about the virtues of the Old Town Triangle. Mr. Angle passed away in 1975.

BILL AND NANCY HYER epitomize the I Will spirit of the nieghborhood. Bill was active in the administration of the Menomonee Club for a number of years and later served as President of the Triangle. Both he and Nancy were ardent supporters of the Art Fair, Nancy chairing the all-important Gates Committee. A trip through Art Fair Program Books from years past reveals many articles by Bill and photographs of the neighborhood that were part of his private collection. Bill worked tirelessly to help the Triangle achieve Landmark status.

BERT RAY AND MARY GEHR. Bert Ray was one of the city's most widely respected graphic designers. His wife, Mary Gehr, was a talented artist who exhibited for many years at the Old Town Art Fair. Most of us remember Mary as the quintessential urban gardener. Quiet, gentle, unbelievably intelligent and creative, Mary attracted friends from every walk of life. Her ability to transform a small plot of land into a magical space of green plants and flowers was unparalleled. Whenever magazines wrote to extol the urban gardener, Mary Gehr's name was among the first mentioned. She was a special lady.

MR. AND MRS. O. M. FORKERT, Maurice and Amy, worked tirelessly to improve the quality of life in Old Town. Many Art Fair program books from the 1950s on bear the distinctive advertisement O. M. Forkert and Associates, Graphic Arts Consultant, Design, Typography. Amy was Chair of the Art Fair in 1960-61 and President of the Triangle Association in 1968-69. She served on committees for both the Triangle and the Art Fair, and was the guiding hand behind the publication of the first Old Town Triangle Association Cookbook, *Dawn to Dawn*. Maurice was President of the Triangle Association in 1976-77. Maurice and Amy undertook the Herculean task of studying and documenting each building in the Triangle to determine whether the Triangle should seek Landmark Status. In 1977, when Maurice was President of the Old Town Triangle Association, that status was granted.

PAUL FAHRENKROG AND HIS WIFE DARLENE have been members of the Triangle for more than 30 years. Paul served on the OTTA Board of Directors for six years and was a member of the Planning and Zoning Committee during the time the neighborhood was seeking Landmark designation. Darlene was on the Menomonee Club Board of Directors and was an Old Town Art School instructor for many years. She exhibited at the Art Fair from 1968 through 1988 and designed the Art Fair posters in 1969, 1973, 1980, and 1981. For three years, she served on the Art Fair entry selection jury. The Fahrenkrogs have lived in their Willow Street residence, designed by Paul, since 1968.

HANNAH SUE SAMUELS Throughout her years in Old Town, Hannah Sue was an active member of the Old Town Triangle Association, serving as board member and president, art fair chair, newsletter editor, and neighborhood archivist. Participating artists have fond remembrances of her annual coffee that announced the opening of the Old Town Art

Fair. Hannah Sue was famous for her bloody marys and for the wonderful baked goods prepared especially for her by the late, great chef Louis Szathmery.

PENNY MILLER single-handedly revolutionized the administration of the Old Town Triangle Association in the 1980s. Under her guidance, the office became more professional: records were computerized; day-to-day operations were systematized; and political affiliations were formed that brought the Triangle into a close working relationship with the local and city political establishments. Her business and administrative skills enabled the Art Fair and the Triangle Center to run with an efficiency never-before experienced. We are all richer for Penny's tenure in Old Town.

DON NELTNOR. Who can forget the sight of Don in his wide-brimmed hat strolling the neighborhood, mentally assessing its well-being? He was the Association's chief critic and its staunchest cheerleader. He advised us, chastised us, and shared with us. During Art Fair, he took on every imaginable task from setting up equipment to collecting and counting the proceeds, and he did them all well. He was a presence we all felt and sorely miss.

DIANE GONZALEZ is one of the Triangle's greatest assets. In 1986-87, Diane served as Art Fair Chair. She was a member of the Triangle Board of Directors from 1990-1999 and on many OTTA and Art Fair committees. Diane is Old Town's resident historian and preservationist. Whenever anyone has a question about Old Town's past, Diane is the first source to whom they turn for information. Some years ago, Diane was recognized by the Illinois Landmarks Commission for her outstanding work in the area of neighborhood preservation. As Art Fair Chair (1986-87), Diane introduced the idea of commemorating the Art Fair with T-shirts. Since then, each fair has had its distinctive poster image or logo stamped on the shirts.

DAN BALDWIN. Every neighborhood should be lucky enough to have a Dan Baldwin. Dan is the epitome of community activism. President of the Triangle Association from 1996-1998, Dan received a commendation from the Mayor of the City of Chicago and the City Council. The Resolution praised Dan for: (1) his involvement and leadership throughout the Old Town community, (2) spearheading the drive for the new playground and recreation area at the LaSalle Language Academy, and (3) serving, with Justine Price, as a prime mover in transforming the old bus turnaround at Clark and Wisconsin Streets into a neighborhood plaza that will serve as a gateway to the landmark Old Town community.

NORMAN BAUGHER. Norman personifies Old Town art and creativity. This talented artist's first service to the community was as an Art Fair thug. In the days before Halls brought equipment to the Fair site, the thugs carried all of the equipment used in the Fair to the various gates, the auction, the food court, and the artists' booths. He graduated to the exalted position of Art Fair Chair for 1998-1999. He has designed the Art Fair posters, program book covers and interiors, and T-shirts since 1988. He developed a logo for Art Fair 2001, which is imprinted on all stationery, cards, and publicity pieces for the Fair. In the last year of the century, he created a design image that has become the official logo for all Triangle publications.

Photographer, Charles Hughes

OUR OLD TOWN, NORTHWEST CORNER
OF NORTH AVENUE AND WELLS STREET, 1945

CHAPTER FOURTEEN

ENVOI

OTTA archive, Chicago, 1871

We end pretty much the way we began. There was a time, long ago, when German settlers placed cabbages and cottages in a dried-up swamp and called it home. When streetcars clanged up and down Wells Street, milk was delivered door to door in large metal containers, and cows and chickens roamed through back yards. When James Beverly, Joe Vitale, Paul Angle, and others formed a little neighborhood organization, called it the Old Town Triangle Association, and vowed to improve the quality of life for its members. When hands were not glued to computer keyboards, cash did not come out of automated teller machines, and life's everyday needs could not be ordered via the Internet. When a 25-cent donation got you into an art fair displaying magical things like home-baked cakes, crocheted potholders, and sequins on heaven only knows what. When Piper's Bakery gave free cookies to the likes of such neighborhood children as Johnny Weismuller, and Francis Chapin worked away in his Menomonee Street studio on some of the most glorious drawings of the period. When men and women got off their buses and walked up narrow little streets to balloon-frame cottages or Victorian-style brick houses that had been built once upon a time.

Come to think about it, maybe once upon a time was not so different from now. Piper's Bakery is gone, but Breadsmith on Wells Street gives fabulous fresh samples free to anyone who walks through the door. Residents get off buses and trains and walk the same narrow streets to balloon-frame cottages or Victorian-style houses unchanged on the outside, but gloriously rearranged inside. Local artists are busy creating masterpieces in their studios on Willow, Lincoln Park West, Crilly Court, and Wells Street. And though the requested donation to the Art Fair has increased from 25 cents to five dollars, there is still magic inside awaiting the strollers.

FRIENDS FOREVER, THE CHILDREN OF OLD TOWN — 1871

FRIENDS FOEVER, THE CHILDREN OF OLD TOWN — 2001
GRETA BALDWIN, DEVIN BOOTH, CAROLINE BALDWIN

Lucy Baldwin

In this new millennium, most of us in the Old Town Triangle are living our happily ever after lives. And we readily join Paul Angle, Don Herbert, Christopher Porterfield, Bill Hyer, and all the others who were here, not so long ago, in saying, "We wouldn't live anywhere else."

OUR OLD TOWN, THE NEXT GENERATION.
MARIKO, SAMMI AND MADDIE, AND ALEX.AS
SEEN BY THEIR PARENTS

Part Three

CHAPTER FIFTEEN

OUR OLD TOWN —
A Selective Anthology from the Pens of Those Who Loved Her

O*ld Town has been home to many authors, journalists, artists, architects, and craftsmen since it shed its Cabbage Patch designation. They have left us with their impressions of and love for the neighborhood. This literary supplement represents only a few of the accolades that have been bestowed on our community in the past 50 years.*

The Old Town Triangle

PAUL M. ANGLE, 1954
Renowned Lincoln scholar and Director of the Chicago Historical Society

Every now and then I awake in the morning, glance at the clock, and indulge in a smug reflection. "Right now," I say to myself, "several thousand poor devils in Glenview or Hinsdale or Beverly Hills are breaking their necks to catch a train." Then I take a short nap, wipe the sleep from my eyes, enjoy a leisurely breakfast, and arrive at work at the same time as the commuters who left their homes while I was still in bed.

The first advantage of the Triangle is that it's close in — 20 minutes from the Loop, and half that time from the North Michigan Avenue section where many of our people work.

And that's an advantage for the whole family as well as for its working members. Do you hanker for a play or for the symphony? Have dinner at home, allow a half-hour, at most, for transportation, and pity all those who are worrying about whether the affair will be over soon enough for them to catch the 10:35. You have no concern with suburban trains or with heavy traffic. You will be home before the 10:35 escapes the city limits.

And at home — you won't have to pay more than a few of the penalties of city living for the conveniences you enjoy. Noise, for example. There is little through traffic in the Triangle, and darkness usually brings a stillness broken only by the friendly sound of St. Michael's chimes, or in bad weather, by the distant croaking of the fog horns of the water cribs. There are trees on our streets, many gardens, though small, in the yards, and Lincoln Park and Lake Michigan are only minutes away. Loneliness— Not in the Triangle. It's hard to walk a block without meeting a first-name friend, and anyone who wants to bring together a good-sized party of congenial people can do so on a half-hour's notice without going beyond a 200-yard radius. Yet in the Triangle, neighborliness doesn't mean nosiness. People respect each other's privacy. If you come home from work with your heart set on an evening of reading, you can be sure that no one will interrupt you, at least without a telephone call to make sure that even a brief visit will not be an intrusion. That's only good manners, of course; but how many of us, in living elsewhere, haven't been subjected to frequent fractures of the code?

In the Triangle, moreover, there is respect for an individual's interests. If, though an amateur, you prefer to struggle with palette and brush, or study French in preference to watching television, no one is going to make side remarks. Conversely, if you prefer a few hours on a bar stool you won't be charged with the proclivities of a stevedore. And even if you stay on that bar stool longer than you should, your neighbors will not be unduly censorious. They'll merely ask that you be equally indulgent.

Which brings us to the subject of conveniences. The Triangle has many — meat markets, bake shops, groceries, restaurants, shoe repair shops, dry cleaners, and drug stores. We don't pretend to be a shopping center, but we do assert that it's a handy thing not to have to walk more than a block when you suddenly realize, at 9:00 p.m., that you're down to your last cigarette.

Of course, we are not without some disadvantages. We have dirt. We have soot. We have more automobiles than garages, and some of our streets are too narrow for present-day traffic. We have a few juvenile hoodlums, and some adults who don't know the difference between an alley and a garbage can. But all in all, the Triangle means pleasant, comfortable living. I wouldn't by preference, live anywhere else in Chicago.

Old Town—Present

DON HERBERT (MR. WIZARD) 1955
Triangle resident and well-known TV personality

My wife and I choose to live in Old Town because it's a small town in a big city. There are many contrasts here. It's fascinating. There's the built-in stimulation of living close to the heart of the second largest city in the United States. A trip to the theatre, the Art Institute, or to a business meeting in a downtown office building is a 10-minute ride. And, with all this convenience, here in Old Town, there's a sort of quiet tempo to living with no crowds, no traffic headaches.

When the weather forecast in summer reads cooler near the lake, that's us. We're near enough to take the kids and the dog for a romp through Lincoln Park or to stroll along the lakefront. And the busy Outer Drive is close by if we, for some reason, want to make a quick exit out of the city.

Our kids have a nodding acquaintance with the bears and camels at Lincoln Park Zoo. The family life of Sinbad and his brother gorillas is as much a topic of dinner table conversation as the domestic pets of neighborhood children.

The pavements are bustling with the business of city life, like any city neighborhood, but in the quiet patios in back of the houses, Old Towners sun themselves or relax in the shade with a lemonade. Deck chairs and beach umbrellas are standard equipment here where leisure is not a project but part of everyday living.

This community is essentially one of professional people with a living to earn. Friends and interests are scattered over wide areas, but neighborly chats are also part of the Old Town personality.

Our neighbors are interesting people. They include a writer, lawyer, salesman, television performer, painter, historian, architect, doctor, newspaper columnist, antique dealer, business executive, drama critic, city official, interior decorator, nurse, radio director, policewoman, and advertising account executive.

There is a neighborly exchange of friendliness, but these are not people who are likely to pop into one's kitchen unannounced. In neighborhood efforts, there is enthusiastic cooperation. No better examples of this can be found than the Menomonee Boys Club, often cited as a model community project, and the annual outdoor fair, which is so successful that other cities send delegations to study it.

The spirit of the community finds its best expression, perhaps, in the Triangle Association. Our neighbors are proud of Old Town and formed the association to preserve it. One of the oldest sections of the city, its buildings are lovingly kept up. And where else in Chicago can you find such militant pride in the blooming window boxes and carefully planted yards and patios?

Too, there is an atmosphere of individuality here. Many of the houses are from the time of the Chicago Fire and have the fine touches of early craftsmanship. Have you noticed the doors, especially? Some of them are handcrafted, carved, and etched with a care you find rarely on this side of the 20th century. Another contrast: inside, many houses are ultra modern. Even the alleys are decorated here in Old Town. One friend of ours has a shocking pink garbage can. Another has a coral-colored back gate.

There is no arty crowd, although we certainly have artists. It's not Greenwich Village circa 1928 Bohemian type living. There's time, and room, and air, and an unpressured style of living that's friendly to families. We have our share of kids roller skating or playing ball in the street (cars drive slower here because our streets are short and narrow) and there are bicycles and baby carriages in evident plenty.

We'd like to think that our kids will grow up with broader horizons for having lived in Old Town.

The Bells of St. Michael's

PAULA ANGLE, 1956
Chicago journalist and daughter of Paul Angle

F*unera planto, fulmina frango, Sabbath pango*
Excita lentos, dissipo ventos, paco cruentos

I mourn death, I disperse the lightening, I announce the
Sabbath, I rouse the lazy, scatter the winds, I appease the
bloodthirsty.

Whenever possible, an essayist should introduce his subject with a phrase
from the Latin. It gives his remarks a depth, a profundity of learning, and
a certain cachet that they otherwise might not possess. So we are grateful
that an earlier writer at some undetermined date gave the above summary
of the subject matter in this piece, which is mostly about the bells of St.
Michael's, an audible tradition of the Old Town Triangle.

According to this tradition, newly coined for the purposes of this
article, Chicagoans residing within the sound of St. Michael's bells are
Old Towners. This tradition bears a strong resemblance to the definition
of Cockneydom, Any person born within the sound of the Bow Bells, the
bells of St. Mary-le-Bow, Cheapside, is a Cockney, a Londoner, pure and
simple. (Bow Bells, another tradition has it, lured Dick Whittington, runaway apprentice, back from Highgate to become Lord Mayor of London.)

But about St. Michael's bells...those who like to imagine black-
cassocked figures tugging on ropes at quarter-hour intervals will be disappointed to hear that the bells are controlled by electricity. When originally
cast, by the McShane Bell Foundry, and installed just after the Great
Chicago Fire, the bell changes were rung by hand.

There are four bells. The two smallest ring the quarter hours. The
largest (two and one-half tons) rings the hour. The middle-sized bell
strikes the Angelus at 6:00 a.m. and is tolled for funerals. More statistics:
the bells are hung 170 feet from the ground, 30 feet below the clock dials,
which are 12 feet across.

Statistics, however, are not sustenance for the imaginative. Let's
take a cue from a local city editor, known for coining Goldwynisms. On

the eve of Lincoln's birthday, a few years ago, he pointed out to his feature writers that stories about Lincoln were well worn. We need some new anecdotes about Lincoln, he allowed. We need some new traditions for our bells. Here are some old stories, just as examples.

Wicked spirits have always been afraid of bells. A ferryman in Holstein got a hatful of gold from a boatload of emigrating dwarfs because they couldn't endure the bells of Holstein any longer. Another bell, also in Germany, was about to be melted down by invaders wanting to make weapons of the metal when the bell began to sweat blood and the ravagers were scared off. It is said of Ireland's St. Mura's bell that a person could cure any ailment if liquid were drunk from its lip.

These examples from the past won't do. Somehow they simply do not fit our case. If Old Towners or Art Fair guests have any suggestions, let's have them, please.

A Sense of History, More or Less

HERMAN KOGAN, 1959

Perhaps I have been unduly remiss in my role as a writer about Chicago, but if any of the professional historical-site outfits has designated Old Town a likely area for plaques and markers, then I have not yet heard of it. You know the kind: Here peace pipes were first smoked with a band of hostile native Americans, there Long John Wentworth paused for a draft of ale when he strode barefoot into town in 1836, on this spot, here a first church, there a first council hall, and so on and so on.

However laggard we consider the plaque-and-marker people, we who are chauvinistic about Old Town (and are there any dwelling here who are not?) have our own sense of history about the place. In purely objective moments, we may be compelled to admit that the official affixers of historical monuments have a point, technically speaking, but we have our own treasuries of historical fact, lore, and memorabilia (and some trivia), and we cherish them all, however unimportant they may seem to the site-pickers, and on all fitting occasions we may yearn to pass on our knowledge to visitors and outlanders.

Old Town's first name was "The Cabbage Patch." This was back in the 1850's and 60's, when scores of truck gardens and cow pastures dotted the area. Toward the east, extending northward from what is now North Avenue, there then stretched a large, uninhabited area of trees and scrub vegetation; part of it was hacked down around 1840 to become one of the city's first cemeteries. An alderman named Lawrence Proudfoot battled vociferously for some 20 years to have this acreage transformed from a place of death to a place of life, and in 1864, he finally won his case. Most of the graves were moved elsewhere, and the tract became the first sector of what is now the vast and verdant Lincoln Park. If you wander over that way, you will find two remnants of the ancient cemetery. In the Couch mausoleum, near the Chicago Historical Society building, are interred Ira Couch, owner of the famed Tremont House, and members of his family (a series of lawsuits kept it where it is today). At the foot of Wisconsin Street stands the Kennison boulder, where lies David Kennison, the last survivor of the Boston Tea Party, who died in 1852 at the age of 115.

The Cabbage Patch was wiped out in the Great Fire of 1871. All buildings were destroyed. If you want to cheat a little in the interests of satisfying your historical curiosity, you can walk over to 2121 North Hudson Avenue, outside Old Town limits, and see the only structure in the general area that did survive.

Old Town still retains the architectural guise that it took on in the years immediately after the Great Fire. Notable Chicagoans, burned out of neighborhoods to the south, built anew here. Some of their homes were baroque and barnlike, crammed with gingerbread inside and out. Others looked like Swiss chalets, or were of a style once described by a critic as "steamboat architecture vintage." You can glimpse some of these in the 200 block of Eugenie Street (a tree-lined thoroughfare named for the daughter of Frederick William Wolf, one of the town's distinguished brewers). Especially worth a second look is the elaborately carved structure at No. 221; it was once the mansion of Thomas J. Webb, the coffee merchant. In those years, there arose the rambling home of the restaurateur Philip Henrici at Lincoln Avenue and Wisconsin Street, and there it still stands. And on Lincoln Park West (then Franklin Street), Frederick Wacker, in the year after the Fire, built a large and rather flamboyant home at No.1838 and a dainty carriage house in the back. The latter was moved up front where his son Charles Wacker, one of Chicago's later developers, grew up and married. Lincoln Park West has some other old houses, notably that in which Paul Angle lives (1802) on the corner of Menomonee, the Tonk House at No. 1817, and another at 1835 (the old number, 709, still etched on its front, represents the former address, 709 Franklin Street). Of historical interest on this Street too, are the residences extending from No. 1826 through 1834; these were the creations of no less an American immortal than Louis Sullivan. He built them for the Halsted family in 1884, fully five years before his masterpiece, the Auditorium opened on Michigan Avenue.

No history, full or fleeting, of Old Town can overlook the Crilly contributions. In 1877, Daniel F. Crilly, a South Side contractor, bought land bound by Wells Street, North Park Avenue, Eugenie Street, and St. Paul Avenue (then Florimond Street). He cut a one-block north-south street through the middle of the property, logically labeled it Crilly Court, and built apartment houses on the east side, naming them for his children—Isabelle, Oliver, Erminnie, and Edgar. An early Crilly tenant was George K. Spoor, the "S" of the pioneer Essanay Film Company, king of the moviemakers when Hollywood was only a scrub patch on Los Angeles' outskirts. Eugene Field also lived for a time in a Crilly Court dwelling.

There is much historical miscellany in Old Town. Eugenie Park, the green patch at Eugenie and Wells, was once the site of Zahner's tavern of the post-Fire vintage, with a noble mahogany bar, a ladies' parlor, and the most complex jangly mechanical piano in town. The Plaza Theater on North Avenue...was for decades a major vaudeville house, its attractions ranging from slapstick comics and acrobats to Ruth St. Denis and Ted Shawn. LaSalle School was an educational showplace when it opened its doors in 1880, its present playground lush with grass and its first principal, Homer Bevens, a vigorous fellow who often burst into eighth-grade classrooms to entertain startled students with selections from Thoreau's Walden. Where the Lincoln Hotel now stands were once the headquarters of the snooty Lincoln Cycling Club. ...Gymnasts and musclemen of the Turn Gemeinde whirled and gyrated and stooped and squatted in the large building on the east side of Wells Street and St. Paul Avenue. And isn't it intriguing to know that on the lot at North Park Avenue and Eugenie Street, there stood circa 1886, one of the city's largest dress-trimming factories; that the Menomonee Boys' Club was once a popular bowling alley; and that one of the things for kids to do in the 1880's, when cable cars replaced the horse cars on Wells Street, was to tie tin cans to a rope, then tie the rope to the car so that the can got snarled between the tracks and caused all kinds of distress to cable, car, conductor, and choleric customers.

Old Town: The Pickle and the Wobs

GEORGE MURRAY, 1958
Old Town resident and reporter for the Chicago American

Try to tell a stranger about Old Town and you'll find words fail. That's because it's a state of mind, quite as much as a section of the city. The area is an anomaly. Though rich in intellectuals, appreciative as well as creative, it is basically a community of home-owning burghers. Foreign cars and convertibles rub bumpers with conservative two-doors. Strains from FM radios clash with the blare of TV sports announcers. Old Town's men feel at ease in beards and berets; its women in paint-stained jeans and smocks. Yet its churches do a land-office business. One resident terms it a combination of Greenwich Village and the PTA. There's a live and let live atmosphere in the Triangle. It goes deeper than the shrill screams for tolerance one hears so much these days.

The physical history of this neighborhood is as easy to trace as its outline on a map—North Avenue, Clark Street, Ogden Avenue. Its philosophical roots aren't as easily discerned. It will shock those who think radical comes from the Russian rather than the Greek to hear that Old Town grew out of early Chicago radicalism. The progression was Wobs to Udell's; Udell's to Pickle, the Pickle to Near North, the Near North to Old Town. I'll explain the whole thing starting with the Wobs.

In 1905, the labor movement was a tame dragon slinking at Samuel Gompers' heels. Along came the Wobs, so hot they set its insides afire. The Industrial Workers of the World, they called themselves. Some said they were red; others swore they were just red, white, and blue. They organized in Chicago. Their initials, I.W.W., led to their being called Wobblies. They shortened it to Wobs and the name stuck.

Most trade union leaders just want to collect dues. Not the Wobs. They had a sense of mission. They wanted to educate the working stiff. To do so, they wrote songs—simple parodies on popular melodies. In horrible rhyme schemes, these painted the bosses in terrible hues. The Wobs did more. They got out pamphlets for the working man. These dealt with history and economics in terms as primitive as their song parodies.

A whole nation was reassessing its views of economics. A new crop of writers turned to the field. Frank Norris, Theodore Dreiser, Upton Sinclair dissected financial and industrial titans in novels; Ray Stannard

Baker and Ida M. Tarbell, in muckraking magazine articles. It was a period of literary ferment.

Since there was a demand for such radical literature, a bookstore came into being to handle it. This was Udell's at 818 N. Clark Street. Jack Jones, a Wobbly organizer, put $300 into the shop. It was called The Radical Bookshop. It dealt in ideas, as well as books. Situated in the old German Turnverin Hall, it was a store in front and a stage in back. Chicago had theater as never before or since. A troupe of unpaid actors played like a stock company. They put on a new bill every week, usually introducing a playwright new to the city. The Studio Players rehearsed Ibsen while playing Strindberg, rehearsed Hauptmann while playing Schnitzler. The stage was nothing but a raised platform, but the illusion was there. Many who acted on it were heard from in later days. Melvyn Hesselberger is now known as Melvyn Douglas. Ralph Bellamy is playing Broadway in Sunrise at Campobello, Frank McHugh is perennially cast as a comic.

The Radical Bookshop put on street dances, among other things. (Two young newspapermen who patronized them were Ring Lardner and Carl Sandburg.) Naturally, these dances drew the old Wobs. Big Bill Haywood attended, and so did Jim Larkin, who later was to win a name in Irish politics.

The bookstore got into so many activities that Jack Jones and others decided to incorporate. Thus, in 1916, the Dill Pickle Club was born. The not-for-profit state charter was issued in March. It told the original twelve members they could promote arts, crafts, and literature. In June, the club found refuge in a stable in Hogan's Alley at the foot of Pearson Street. Later, Jones moved from Hogan's Alley to Tooker Alley, at the rear of 862 N. State Street, where Slim Brundige now runs his College of Complexes. Eventually, the Dill Pickle Club was to extend right through from State to Dearborn Street. Its buildings enclosed a delightful patio garden.

Between 1916 and 1932, Jones—Canadian by birth, and a miner by trade—brought to this free speech forum the leaders of world thought. Talk of Chicago's post World War I intellectual ferment, and you have to mention the Dill Pickle Club. It was the mecca for everyone, the center of Chicago's avant garde.

It made the Near North Side a midwest Greenwich Village. Ruth St. Denis and Ted Shawn danced at the Pickle. Frank Lloyd Wright talked there. Harriet Monroe ran poetry evenings. Every shade of radical was welcome, be he—or she—Second, Third, or Fourth International. The Bolsheviks generally lost in debate. A dozen books were written there. The Pickle provided a piano for composers, a stage for dancers, a gallery for the display of artists' work. It had shops of every description. Visitors from everywhere, coming to Chicago, wanted to see the place.

That's how the Near North Side got to be the home of Chicago's bohemians. They settled east of Clark Street, from Grand to North Avenue.

The Pickle closed during the Depression. The people it had attracted, with nothing to hold them as industry advanced from the river, moved on north. The artists and the craftsmen, the doers and the thinkers, and those who just like to talk about it settled north of North Avenue.

That's the way Old Town, peopled by good German burghers, came to be host to artists. High-income intellectuals moved in because they liked the neighborhood's tree-lined streets, Old World charm, and casual atmosphere. As state of mind or as church-going community, Old Town is an invigorating area. It isn't easy to put its charm into words.

Old Town Architecture

JOHN A. HOLABIRD, JR. 1964
Noted Chicago architect, currently painting and studying art at the Old Town Art Center

Buildings in the Triangle area are characterized by a grand and glorious mixture of styles and building skills now called Victorian. They borrow from the French (mansard roofs), from the Italian Renaissance (arched windows, pilasters, and loggias), from the Gothic (pointed windows, articulated structure, and stained glass), and from American and American immigrant know-how in building with brick masonry and white pine. To the residents of the area, the Old Town architectural character means houses and flats, which because of generous and stately proportions, of ample storage areas, of pleasant and warm relationships between tall, narrow windows and enclosing walls, and of charming details of wood, plaster, and metal in mantles, door trim, moldings, and banisters, seem much more attractive and livable than anything that recent builders have been able to produce. To the architect, it becomes more and more evident that the Victorian builders had a real feeling for urban architecture; that these houses, despite and even because of their peculiar and ornate embellishments, made a strong statement of belonging to a city and expressing their function as residences. They look good by themselves and they look good in groups; they produce neighborhoods and street facades. In absolute fact, they make a city.

There are a number of qualities which Old Town buildings have in common which assist in creating good urban architecture. First, and probably most important, they share a common scale. They are all about the same height and are all packed closely together (built by developers in packages and rows). Suburban subdivisions are all low, but they rarely suggest a community. The buildings in the Triangle seem right and proper for the person walking in the street, climbing the stair, and living within—high enough to establish a façade, low enough to see the sun and sky. The lots are used fully so that little is left for lawns and gardens along the street. Land was dear and it was economical to build one house cheek to jowl with the next. There are, of course, endless varieties in exact height and width, but the total resultant is a harmonious backdrop.

Second, there is the common quality of materials and detail. Almost all Old Town architecture is wood or brick with combinations of stone, of ironwork, and occasionally of stucco. The wood buildings shot up in the 1870's and 1880's after the Chicago Fire as builders invented and exploited the lightweight "balloon" framing system of two by four wall studs and two by twelve floor joists. In the 1890's and early 1900's, the typical brick three-story row house appeared throughout the area. Then, a third wave of building took place in the first quarter of this century. Such structures include various and nondescript apartment buildings, hotels, and garages which had lost the earlier inventiveness of the Victorian Period but added no charm of their own, contributing only drabness. Thankfully, there are few of these.

The wood and brick buildings were constructed at a time when masons and carpenters took pride in their skill and versatility. Their buildings gave pleasure to the neighborhood, here a finely wrought balustrade or a cunningly executed entrance door—there some intricate scroll work on the porch, ornamental lintels over the windows, or handsome brackets along the roof line, or a satisfyingly ornate cornice or roof structure. From a distance, one saw only the material and the color, but as one came closer, walking by or climbing up the stairs, the smaller and more sophisticated details could be absorbed and appreciated. In the present day of massive boxes of buildings with one identical geometric elevation on all sides, it is exhilarating to find one surprise after another simply by walking down an Old Town street.

Third, Old Town profits from a lovable and disorderly city plan. We live in an era now of standards—proper widths of streets, proper setbacks, proper front, rear, and side yards, and all such hocus-pocus. It is refreshing to find, therefore, how well Old Town still functions with streets and lots of all widths, going nowhere. Streets are short. They start and stop. But one street's ending stops the eye, encloses the space, then starts an entirely new vista in a different sense. It is difficult to park and to speed under these conditions, but then…which is more important? Fourth, Old Town buildings have a quality of age. Even the drab apartments of the last building era some forty years ago have a quasi-dignity. Very few bright developers have felt compelled to establish outposts of shiny glass, aluminum, and steel in this aging area. The good new buildings, such as the one on Eugenie Street designed by architect Harry Weese, look grown up and mature already and have joined the fraternity of Old Town Urban Architecture.

As you walk through Old Town, try to keep in mind some of the common qualities which the Victorian buildings share—of scale, of materials, details, unrigid plan, and age. My favorite streets are pieces of all of them: St. Paul, Crilly Court, Wisconsin, Menomonee, Willow, North Park;...see if you agree. Notice how well most owners have mastered the maintenance and long-term care of the "character."

The wood buildings have suffered the most. Wood needs constant paint, and to save money, some owners have sold their houses down the river by covering the fine old lines with brick tar paper and artificial stone siding—the end! Brick homes are easier to maintain. You will notice all sorts of good approaches. In some cases, the owners have had the brick cleaned or painted so that the materials look spanking new. The destroyers of brick houses have generally been the thoughtless entrepreneurs who have felt that if a fickle public likes this "old stuff" so much, why not throw in some fancy New Orleans iron work, some phony New England window boxes, some cottage-y shutters...? The public is then supposed to love them even more. The cuteness is abysmal.

Old Town, now in the throes of urban renewal, is undoubtedly in for a fourth period of building activity. Hopefully the lessons to be learned from its unknown Masters of the Past will not be tossed away.

Francis Chapin, Man of Good Will

SARAJANE WELLS, 1964-65

Chicago has a reputation, there's no doubt about it; in the science of meanings, the work reputation leans toward intra dignitatem. Reputation is an overworked word and frequently quite painful to the ears of Chicago's more sensitive citizens. But if we can forget the opprobrious past, just for a while, and ignore the present too, if we can forget the arrant disdain of syndicate activities, the governmental tolerance of things shabby and sometimes downright base, if we can forget what much of the world considers to be Chicago's only reputation, then let us look about us at the bright ring of beauty, creativity, and pure talent offered by men of good will.

Some of that talent settled in Old Town long ago. Some of it moved away, seeking the gold or the glory or the comfort of new surroundings; but some of the best, the very best, stayed on in the heart of the Old Town Triangle. Our neighborhood is warmly proud of the artists we can claim as our very own. We cherish them and hope to keep them here. If such an attitude is chauvinistic, perhaps it can be forgiven for its very humanism.

Among the artists we hold most dear, none is better known or more completely accepted for his creative approach and undisputed talent than Francis Chapin, an Old Town resident for many years. Chape and his wife, Vivian, an artist of stature in her own right, live and work in their studio home on Menomonee Street. Both exhibit their work at the Old Town Art Fair. Collectors seek them out and a knowing public respects them.

Francis Chapin is sought, too, by colleges and universities when a Resident or Lecture post is open to a visiting artist. Just this year, he joined the faculty of Stetson University for a term as artist-in-residence, then went on to Columbus, Georgia for the Visiting Artists Program sponsored by the American Federation of Arts and Museums. He is listed in Who's Who in America. He has a wealth of credits in teaching, in commissions, in exhibitions, in awards, and purchase prizes both here and abroad. A graduate of Washington and Jefferson College and the Art Institute of Chicago, he has traveled and painted in France, England,

Holland, Italy, Spain, Portugal, and Mexico. He was Artist-in-Residence at the American Academy in Rome in 1960-62.

A list of Francis Chapin's exhibitions, both group and one-man shows, is long and impressive. And, we are still remembering that this man of good will, this man of abundant creativity and talent, lives and works within the area of the Old Town Triangle. He exhibits permanently at the Fairweather-Hardin Gallery, 141 East Ontario Street, Chicago; and his work is often available at the Old Town Art Center, 1714 N. Wells Street. This is the local gallery sponsored as a civic endeavor by the Triangle Association, the organization that has presented the Art Fair for 15 consecutive years.

How many honors can one man receive? We've mentioned only a few of the seemingly endless list. Francis Chapin has work in the permanent collections of the Art Institute of Chicago, the Metropolitan Museum in New York, the Brooklyn Museum, and the list goes on. His work at the Art Institute of Chicago includes two watercolors, two oils, a gouache, and a superb collection of lithographs in the Institute's Print Department. In 1949, he received an Art Institute First Prize for an oil, Black Bull, which was reproduced, with an article in Time Magazine, June 1950. This painting is now in the collection of the Chicago Athletic Association.

The Chapins, with their young son Todd, spend the summers on Martha's Vineyard in Edgartown, where they built a summer studio near the sea. Here, they both paint and show, and help to keep things going at the Martha's Vineyard Art Association, which has a charming gallery on the Edgartown waterfront. And, we are still remembering that Francis Chapin, between tours and travel and teaching, lives with his family and gives of his talent within the limits of the Old Town Triangle area.

A Chape achievement of interest to other artists, as well as to those of us who only stand and admire, is the result of his work with Ramon Shiva, color chemist, wherein he compounded the Chapin neutrals for the Artist's oil palette.

Through the years, admirers have pinned titles on this tall, blue-eyed man who quietly goes about his studio and his neighborhood, working and creating the beauty which deserves such title-pinning, and we quote, one of America's best-loved artists, dean of Chicago painters, and one of America's most creative colorists.

How now, semanticists, the meaning of reputation? Where, in the science of meanings, do we fit the Chicago of art in its most delightful sense? Just a few weeks ago, the pen of a distinguished critic, writing now for a well-known newspaper, demoted Chicago from Second City to Third City. Then, a week later, we were admonished to hurry about and rustle up another art museum. Reputation oh, reputation. Just for a while, we are forgetting the disgrace of crime, injustice, and apathy (for which artists could not fashion, Chicago-style, if they tried)..so why Third instead of Second? May the late and gifted A. J. Liebling rest in his tragically early grave.

 The Old Town Art Fair, spread upon a tiny patch of land between the towers of the Third city's stage-set façade and the transience of beleaguered Ogden Avenue, has been a unique force for talent and time, for artist and buyer, for old neighbors and new ideas. Francis Chapin, respected as he is, is just one example of the men and women of good will, artists in many fields, who have peopled our area and exhibited their considerable talents to an eager public. Those artists who actually live within the Triangle itself, and whose work is exhibited in the current Art Fair, cannot be classified as second or third, nor can their associates who live without the boundaries, but who share equally important roles in such an endeavor. Just as a mental exercise, study the list of exhibitors actually living on the tiny patch of ground called the Triangle: Franz Altschuler, George Botich, Eleanor Coen, Francis and Vivian Chapin, Fred Cunningham, Nita Engle, Dorris Gammon, Mary Gehr, Paula Gerard, Bacia Gordon, James Holley, Max Kahn, David and Esther Landis, Hester Murray, Quintin Neal, Bill Olendorf, Mary Peterson, Juliet Rago, Ralph Rapien, Frank Vavruska, Mehigan Weeden, Robert Wilson, Jane Young. And near neighbors, artists who live within paint box throw of the tiny patch of land: Robert Appel, Gunther Aron, Catherine Cajandig, James Cassell, Eldon Danhausen, James Robert Estes, Bill Frank, Madge Friedman, Peter Gold, Nancy Hawke, Alice Lauffer, Ruth Linnell, Don Luck, Rudolph Pen, Judy Morris Petacque, Jasper and Michael San Fratello, James Swann.

 Where an artist lives is not a measure of his talent, of course, and the above names were not compiled for any such reason, you may be sure. Other noteworthy Art Fair exhibitors hail from points north, south, and west, But, isn't it a comforting sign to those who believe a city's reputation is not made of gangs and guns, of blight and blasphemy; to know we harbor such a lovely roster? How can a city be classed Third when we have, close to our homes, as well as our hearts, a Mary Gehr, a David Landis, a Francis Chapin?

Chicago has, indeed, a reputation. It is time, we think, to apply the best meaning to the word, the meaning that reflects the efforts of men and women of good will?

· · · · · ·

Francis Chapin died the next year, in 1965. Of his passing, Sarajane Wells wrote, …

And Lies Down to Pleasant Dreams…The pictures still exist, but a very special gentleman is gone. Students and fellow artists are richer for having known or worked with Francis Chapin, to have shared his knowledge and his experience, to have watched him create the beauty that critics acclaimed. He gave his counsel to the Triangle Association whenever it was requested and gave generously of his time and his great talent when he was called upon. If one were to seek an epitaph for Chape, the words of Henry Wadsworth Longfellow might well serve: Dead he is not, but departed–for the artist never dies.

Old Town:
A View from the Back Porch

CHRISTOPHER PORTERFIELD,
Correspondent, Time Magazine, 1966

Spring in Old Town is the season when I become an object of curiosity on my own back porch. Particularly around Art Fair time, visitors stroll behind my apartment building, along a bare asphalt passageway that is rather grandiloquently called a court, and look up at me with faces that are questioning, expectant.

They are wondering, I presume, about Old Town and what it's really like to live here. They seem to be looking to me for some sign, some revealing stance or gesture that will answer their curiosity. I often get the feeling that I'm expected to exemplify quaintness or artiness, since many people take these qualities to be the essence of Old Town. If so, then I must be a disappointing figure, sitting quietly with a drink and a book, and doing nothing more quaint than going barefoot.

It's true, that among the back porches I could easily sail my book into from where I sit, some are occupied by a poet, a jazz drummer, a retired Alaskan pioneer, and a graphic artist, as well as several of my fellow journalists. Old Town is home for a lot of creative and unusual people, and they do lend the area a special flavor. But this is not the essence of the place.

Nor would the strollers beneath my porch come any closer to the essence by going over to Wells Street, though there they would certainly find much more that's colorful and even bizarre. "Ah, Old Town," say my suburban and out-of-town friends, and in their eyes is the neon gleam of Wells Street at night. "That's part of it," I hedge, wondering how I can convey to them that another reality lies behind the motley facades of Wells Street—which, in its mixture of the marvelous and the ersatz, has always reminded me of a never-never street on a movie set.

Of course, being so close to all those shops and nightspots is nice, in spite of their tendency to increase the local crime rate and decrease the amount of sleep you can get on weekends. On the whole, proximity to Wells Street is still one of the features of life in Old Town that real estate people call Advantages.

Old Town, in fact, has many such advantages. I can get to my office downtown by bus in ten minutes, for instance, which means, among other things, that on warm spring afternoons, I can easily escape the Loop for a pleasant lunch on my back porch. The North Avenue Beach is within walking distance. And, on weekends, when my wife and I venture out with our toddler son to wander in Lincoln Park to ride a boat or visit the zoo, or relax amid the flowers outside the conservatory, we invariably swear in the name of Daniel F. Crilly that we'd never want to live anyplace else in Chicago.

But these are all benefits that Old Town enjoys geographically, in relation to other things. What would I tell the strollers, what would I show them of the area itself?

I'd pick out no single thing. For Old Town is, to use the name of one of its shops, a gallimaufry, a hodgepodge. One glance at its architecture will confirm that. Renaissance pilasters, Gothic stained glass windows, French mansard roofs, elaborate cornices, even a Swiss chalet. And the things framed in this melange are equally varied: a Buddhist church, a burial stone for a survivor of the Boston Tea Party, a satirical theater, an art center, and so on. The gallimaufry of Old Town is idea for people with serendipity the faculty for accidentally making happy discoveries. With its variety, its intriguingly irregular layout, its short streets and alleys, it's odd byways, and sheltered urban coves. Old Town is full of such discoveries, for those who live here as well as visiting strollers.

What holds it all together and gives it an identity and meaning is this: it is a community. I don't mean a neighborhood, which is merely a separate physical locale and of which there are dozens throughout Chicago. I mean a community in the sense that the common thread of its varied life, the principle of unity in all its diversity, is a kind of shared experience and shared outlook on life that reminds me of a small town, except that it's interwoven with so much that is cosmopolitan and sophisticated in Chicago.

Barry Goldwater was right about one thing, at least. We do all have a pastoral nostalgia for small-town American life. That life may never have existed in the form we imagine, but the idea of it sums up our yearning for an existence that is intimate, simple, and comfortable. I'm sure that my own case of this nostalgia explains why I find it so gratifying to look up and see the spire of St. Michael's above the trees and buildings of Old Town, or to lie in bed and hear St. Michael's bells, and feel almost that I'm in a village.

Old Town offers a way, in an intensely urban setting, to lead a simple and comfortable life without feeling either adrift in a huge and faceless city or smothered in the organized coziness of a suburb.

Within its boundaries, the personal note is dominant. There's an easy, open, back-porch mood that encourages intimacy (but fortunately doesn't compel it). Even the apartment buildings on Crilly Court are named not for things, but for people—the builder's children, in fact: Erminie, Edgar, Oliver, and Isabelle. I like that. In its physical dimensions, Old Town seems built on a human scale as few things are in modern cityscapes. This is what gives its buildings, different as they are from each other, a close relationship with surrounding buildings and the community: their matching small size. And you need only try to wedge into a parking place on Crilly Court or drive down Menomonee to realize that these streets are for pedestrians rather than automobiles.

Old Towners respond to their setting by living with a relish that is individualistic, but at the same time enhances the collective life of their neighbors. This comes out most strongly in their penchant for decoration—the colors they paint their homes, the flowerboxes they hang on their porches, the gardens they cultivate. This year, my next door neighbor is brightening up her garbage can with white polka dots. Modest as some of these touches are, they all show that Old Towners not only want to express their own vitality, but also care about style, about the atmosphere of their homes and their area. Where the sense of community is lacking, you have none of this concern, and you get the dreary, monotonous blankness that characterizes so much of residential America, both rich and poor.

I haven't lived in Old Town long enough to see it change much, though I'm sure it will, I hope it will yield to the future gracefully. Too much bemusement with its past, or even its present, could produce the deadly air of an authentic restoration and turn its residents into curators. As long as Old Town remains a community in spirit, it shouldn't have much to fear from physical change, now even from those shock troops of change, the urban renewal planners. Harry Weese's apartment building at Eugenie and North Park is an elegant example of how the new can blend smoothly into the texture of the old while retaining its own freshness. With the right combination of determination and resilience on the part of its residents, Old Town can absorb change, survive it, and go on evolving with its essence intact.

I suppose it's because that essence is such an elusive, subjective quality that I never would try to answer the implied questions in the face of those strollers. I'd nod, maybe, or smile, then go on reading and wiggling my toes. After all, to really feel the sense of community that makes Old Town what it is, you'd have to do what I'm doing—live here.

The Unknown Old Town Triangle

AMY FORKERT, 1978
Longtime resident, past Art Fair Chair, and Triangle President.

Amy and her husband Maurice were instrumental in achieving Landmark status for the neighborhood.

. . . .

On September 28, 1977, the City Council of Chicago, by unanimous vote, designated the Old Town Triangle an historic landmark district. A great amount of research and documentation of every building in the area had to be undertaken to justify this designation. This search into the past uncovered many more interesting facets of Triangle architectural history.

Superb Iron Work

Almost unnoticed over many years is the magnificent decorative ironwork of outer gates, railings, and fences. Some of these date back to the World's Columbian Exposition of 1893. Others were saved from the claws of the bulldozer by the early pioneers of the Triangle.

Some of the finest iron gates, railings, and posts are in the 1800 block of North Orleans. They came from the 33-room McClurg mansion which stood at 1400 N. Lake Shore Drive. Patterned after a French chateau by Architect Francis Whitehouse, the building was completed in the early 1890's for General A.C. McClurg, president of the largest publishing and wholesale book firm in the Middle West. The house later became the residence of the late George M. Reynolds, at one time chairman of the Continental Illinois Bank. Bringing these superb gates and fences from the Gold Coast to Orleans Street was no easy task. It three to four men to lift a single 450-pound iron post into the concrete foundation.

The variety of design and craftsmanship of these fences is not the product of the South. Many of them originated right here in Chicago. Hinderers' Iron Works of New Orleans remember when they ordered the iron castings from Chicago and other Mid-West cities. It was here where companies had all the ornamental stampings and component parts used by ornamental ironworkers in those days. The eminent architectural art photographer and author, Clarence John Laughlin of New Orleans, in his fascinating book The Personal Eye, says: It is practically unknown that Chicago has more and better wrought iron work than such cities as New Orleans, Charleston, etc. Nor even Chicagoans themselves know this.

Hidden Architectural Values

Many features in Old Town Triangle houses are not visible to the annual Art Fair visitor. Many houses rebuilt after the Chicago Fire of 1871 have double exterior walls with firetraps between the inside and outside walls in order to extinguish smoke and fire. The ashes from the fireplaces were generally collected through the fireproof flues in the basements.

Even the air ducts for wood or coal heating were so well built that later conversions into modern dual heating and air conditioning units have been made with no structural changes and at very low cost.

Inside Triangle homes you will find fantastic decorative elements such as fine cut and colorful stained glass windows, ornate ceiling rosettes and woodwork moldings, parquet floors, marble fireplaces, carved doors, elegant brass hardware, and secret wall safes. Retaining these elements makes these old houses more livable and humane.

The thirty year restoration efforts in the Old Town Triangle have created gracious living close to the city and provide a remarkable example of how a neighborhood sold on itself can regain a long-lost charm.

The Old Town Triangle, A Brief Look Back

BILL HYER, 1986

Today, as you stroll through the thronged streets and the narrow little backways, you might like to know that Old Town's first name was "The Cabbage Patch." Why? Because in the 1850's an abundance of truck gardens bedded in the meadows above the North Avenue city limits. Early settlers, mostly Germans, included Napoleon's Colonel Canda, who came after Waterloo to farm the Cabbage Patch. Soon after, forward-looking William Ogden (who became Chicago's first mayor) and map publishers Rand and McNally began buying land here for development.

All was going well until the Chicago Fire of October 1871 flattened the area. Undaunted, residents quickly rebuilt with mostly simple homes. Industrious parishioners of St. Michael's recreated their church in just a year and three days.

As the neighborhood evolved, Colonel Canda sold his farm to developer Daniel Crilly. Several well-to-do persons, such as Frederick Wacker, built more elaborate digs. The immortal Louis Sullivan built row houses for Ann Halsted five years before his masterpiece; the Auditorium opened on Michigan Avenue. New houses were interspersed with garages, living quarters above for chauffeurs of the wealthy Gold Coast families. These included John Shedd, Chairman of Marshall Field's, and Phillip and Watson Armour. Their garages were the building now occupied by the Triangle Center.

The city was moving. In the 1880's, cable cars replaced the Wells Street horse car line which ended at Wells and Lincoln. And, isn't it intriguing to know that the Menomonee Club was then a popular bowling alley?

Around World War I, Crilly Court became the most fashionable dwelling place in Old Town. There, poet Eugene Filed wrote Little Boy Blue. And when Hollywood was only a scrub patch on Los Angeles' outskirts, Crilly's George Spoor filmed the first Keystone Kops chase along the street that runs through the heart of the Court. Spoor was also known for his many Charlie Chaplin comedies made in Chicago.

For many years, the whole neighborhood woke up to the delightful fragrance of freshly baking bread from Piper's Bakery. Every time a local youngster, like Johnny Weismuller [of early Tarzan fame], bought bread in Piper's glorious interior, they gave him a cookie. Some old timers today still remember when Duchess, Lincoln Park Zoo's restless elephant broke away from her keeper one spring day and made an impromptu tour of Old Town's alleys, leaving in her wake scattered garbage cans and delighted children.

The name Old Town came into use after World War II; the Old Town Triangle Association was founded in 1948. In 1959, the first of the famous flowering trees were planted. More recently, the Old Town Triangle District was named a historical Chicago Landmark and soon after won a well-earned place on the National Register of Historic Places.

Throughout its history, the Triangle has held a steady, irresistible charm. It's a worthy neighborhood. We residents love it here because we know its charm strikes the sight, and its merit wins the soul.

The Old Town Triangle:
an Oral History, 1987

In 1987, under the direction of Jane Durkott, members of the Old Town Triangle Association began work on an oral history of the neighborhood. Seven long-time residents were interviewed by Triangle members before the project was abandoned. The following excerpts from the document provide fascinating insights into the founding of two pioneer religious institutions in the neighborhood: the Midwest Buddhist Temple and St. Michael's Church, and into life in Old Town at mid-century.

Interview with Jim Nishimura on the Founding of the Midwest Buddhist Temple Conducted by Ky Hilliker in February, 1987. Mr. Nishimura was office manager of the Temple at the time and had been associated with the church for 42 years.

KH: I would like to talk to you first about the climate in 1944 when Reverend Kono gathered six or seven people together to form the temple here.

JN: As you may recall, 1944 was still a war year. Due to the panic and hysteria of the war, the government said all Japanese nationals and Japanese-American citizens had to be rounded up and incarcerated in various internment camps. We were herded into stockades under military guard and surrounded by barbed wire. While we were in the camps, many of us who were American citizens and those who were still going to school were given a chance to resume our education by applying for school in the Midwest or on the East coast. No one could return to the West coast because the government feared we might be disloyal.

So, I came here. Reverend Kono also came from a camp in Poston, Arizona. He knew there would be a need for a religious organization since Japanese Americans were coming to Chicago in large numbers and many Japanese American soldiers were being discharged from the service. So he established the Midwest Buddhist temple with six charter members.

Reverend Kono had to report to a security officer whenever the group was going to hold a meeting. Once the temple was established, we started looking around for a facility to rent. We first met in a place called the South Community Hall on Cottage Grove (now Martin Luther King Drive). Our services were held under the supervision of the FBI. We were told to be cautious and tell our congregation to leave by twos and threes to avoid attracting attention, lest people who saw us might think we were having some kind of wartime meeting for saboteurs. That's how sensitive things were in those days.

When we left our camps, our Issei parents told us that if we ever went to Chicago, BE CAREFUL. They had heard about the gangsters in Chicago. Our parents told us we should work to be model citizens, work hard, work honestly, and don't do anything that would bring shame to the rest of the Japanese evacuees living in Chicago. None of us would ever do anything to dishonor our families.

Even in those days, I remember walking along Division and Clark and a lot of young Caucasian kids who didn't understand us would taunt us with racial slurs. Many of them had never seen a Japanese before. At that time, I was young and had a chip on my shoulder. My friend and I wanted to pick a fight with them. But we realized that fighting was not the answer, so we tolerated the slurs. We have this word Gamman, which means if you get slapped on one cheek, turn the other. This is probably one of the reasons we went off to the camps without offering resistance. Did you know that there were 120,000 of us incarcerated without any trial or hearing? Now, we have this thing called redress going on. It is called the Redress Legislation and Civil Liberties Act and is named after the famed Nisei battalion that fought in the European theater.is not the Nisei or the Issei who instigated this action, but our kids who are Sanseis, the third generation. They want to know why we just accepted all these things.

KH: When did you move to North Park and Menomonee?

JN: I first came to Chicago in 1945 because I had applied for a school as an undergraduate student. I was an aeronautical engineer student, so the schools that accepted me were Globe Aircraft and

McDonnell Douglass in Lockport in Lockport and another in St. Louis. Because I had so many friends in Chicago, I came here. I still had to have a sponsor, though, so I would not be a ward of the government. My sponsor was Howard Meadors, a real estate agent and banker. Mr. Meadors had shown Reverend Kono and me buildings all over the near North side area when we came to the building at 1763 N. North Park. We didn't have much money, only what a few Issei members had saved. So, we had to have some income property.

The North Park building looked pretty much the same as it does now. There were apartments on the top three floors. The lower floor was rented by Novo products which just packaged cards and general mailing letters. The ground floor on the north side of the building looked to be a place where we could have our social hall and the south side, which had been a meat packing company, could be converted into a temple hall. So, that's what we did. In the distant past, it was used as a place to keep horse-drawn carriages, and later automobiles. They used to have mechanics in there to do their particular mechanical work. There used to be a lot of mechanics' stalls there. The walls were bricked with glazed tiles and concrete blocks…the floor was all concrete and drain tile because of the garage work. By putting down asphalt tiles, we were able to make some kind of presentable hall there. That is how we got started. At the same time we were having our religious services, we were able to realize some kind of income from the apartments that we rented out to area tenants and a couple of our church members.

KH: Was this around 1950?

JN: 1949, I believe is when the building was purchased and the conversion started.

KH: What was the neighborhood like at that time, and how did they welcome you?

JN: At that time, to our south, was the Menomonee Boys Club. We had a good relationship with them because, at the time, we had to work out a deal with them and the Old Town Triangle Association to hold some of our Sunday School classes in their hall. I remember that some of the early members of the Triangle Association were Amy Forkert, Leigh Sills, and Sue Samuels who were very helpful to us. When they had their first art fair, our being in the community we were asked to join them, which we gladly did. We didn't know what to provide for our participation. Our church was the only one in the area that had immediate access for telephones and washroom facilities. They also thought we might be able to provide some food for the first art fair.

The first art fair offerings were very meager to what we do now. We just had tea and cookies. Later, we got into fried shrimp and rice. From there, we got to the point where we started experimenting with teriyaki chicken (and later into chow mein and rice). The first time we had chicken, we put a concrete block on the sidewalk just north of our building and improvised some charcoal and simple grating there. That was the start of our chicken. It seemed to be a big hit with the neighbors to have the teriyaki.

KH: Would you tell us about the Brotherhood Dinners that took place with the Old Town Triangle Association?

JN: The first one that we had was with Amy Forkert as chairman. Because I was associated with the church, she and I worked out the arrangements. The Bakery Restaurant and Chef Louis catered the food. The hall was filled with Triangle people and that was when they first got to know our congregation and what Buddhism was all about. I think I gave a short talk. Then Maurice Forkert gave some thoughts about his experiences here in Chicago. The second Brotherhood Dinner was headed by Leigh Sills. I remember working with her on that, too.

KH: What about the early Ginza Festivals on North Park?

JN: The present Ginza Festival is our 32nd. In order to have our festival, we had to close off North Park. We built a stage and had to inconvenience the local residents, especially Mr. and Mrs. Paul Angle, whose house butted up against the north end of our stage. For years, they were very, very understanding and thoughtful. When I think about the amount of noise we made constructing the stage and during the three days of the festival, I realize what a great deal we owe to the Angles and the other residents. The old three-floor building right across from our temple was, at that time, owned by Japanese bachelors from whom we purchased it. (It is now owned by Rona Talcott Davis.) We needed a place for the people to eat during the festival, and we used the little garden area adjacent to it.

One fear we had was rain, because then visitors would have to come into our chapel to eat. Our social hall had been converted to the Midwest Buddhist Temple Judo Academy. So in that room, we had many mats and tatami. People would come in and sit around the tatami.

I remember when we first bought that building on North Park, we did not have an adequate kitchen and storage space, so we expanded the kitchen and storage areas. I had to get the permits and go around getting okays from all kinds of residents in the area. It was constructed and used eventually. After we moved to 435 Menomonee, we rented out that first floor to a Lutheran church.

KH: How did you raise the funds to build the temple on Menomonee?

JN: Around 1964-65, we started to think about places to expand because the facilities we had on North Park were inadequate. We had to think about the future, and talk centered around whether to stay in the Triangle area or not. The alternative was to move to the suburbs. We formed a committee to look into the location of a new place. In order to do this, we would need funds to meet this eventual commitment, so we had a finance committee to assist us. We went to a pledge system instead of merely paying $5.00, 10.00, or 20.00 a year. We needed a commitment from each family or individual because, even in those days, construction costs were going to be $1,500,000. For a handful of members, you can imagine how much each one had to pledge.

We also formed a committee to oversee the design and construction of the new facility. We engaged an architect who was Japanese-American. He had studied at the University of Minnesota and studied the renderings of Japanese design with Mr. Hide Arao, who is a Chicago resident. We eventually had a church meeting to decide which design was the best. We had about three designs from competing architects. Arao's design was the one that all church members voted for because it most resembled a typical Japanese temple. The interior design of the chapel was also done by Mr. Arao's firm. We has a local gardener make the garden design.

Surprisingly, through our fortitude and perservance, we were able to pay off our debt far earlier than we anticipated. We have no debt, and our mortgage is free and clear. We still have a pledge system which we use to improve the place and provide operating expenses.

KH: Was this urban renewal land at the time?

JN: Yes, and the city worked with us. When urban renewal came to the area, they came with the intention of closing Ogden Avenue. They had heard we were considering a move to the suburbs and asked us to work with them in their office on Armitage where Alderman Marty Oberman also had his office. The city offered to share in the development, or at least negotiate some of the land for our new site. It worked out fine for us and Urban Renewal, and for the Triangle because we decided to stay here.

I think we made the right choice. I think we have established some stability in the community. Unfortunately, our founder, the Reverend Kono, passed away in 1975, so we had a replacement minister, Reverend Yamohoto, who came from the headquarters in San Francisco. Then we had Reverend Ron Miyamura,who was our minister for several years. When he took another job, we got Reverend Kujo who came from Hawaii. He came in 1981. He impressed upon us the importance of putting some of our benefits back into the community. Once or twice a year, our congregation participates in a clean-up of our building and grounds to beautify the area. This project is done under the supervision of Mr. Henry Koyanagi, a very good gardener.

Jane Durkott Interviews Father Barton, Priest at St. Michael's, in 1985

JD: Who was the original pastor of St. Michael's Church and where did he come from?

FB: His name was Bishop Rulhoff and he came from Baltimore. In those days, our diocese was not known as the Chicago Diocese, but the Baltimore Diocese. When they built the church here, the bishop came all the way from Baltimore by stagecoach in order to bless the church. When he got to St. Michael's, the German people, who pretty well inhabited the area, were standing in front. Bishop Rulhoff said, I am your bishop and I have come to bless your church. The parishioners wouldn't accept him because he was Irish. Thus, Rulhoff had to return to Baltimore, and they sent a German priest, Father Mueller.

JD: St. Michael's has celebrated the centennial of the Redemptorist order coming to this church in 1860. Was that when Father Mueller came?

FB: Yes. Until his arrival, the church was a little place on the corner of Cleveland and North Avenue—a tiny, shabby building. There had been an addition put onto it, near where the first school was located. The population outgrew the building. You know, everything previously stopped at the Chicago River. As a matter of fact, there wasn't much out here. This area came from the Indians. The U.S. government made a treaty with the Indians, and it was partially the government who granted this area to the church.

The parishioners did most of the work building St. Michael's. That's why, after the fire, they were able to rebuild it so quickly. They were laborers during the day and worked on the church in their off hours.

JD: How did the parishioners at that time make a decision to ask the Redemptorists to come to St. Michael's?

FB: The Redemptorists were in the East, and most of the residents from other nations came through New York. There were many Redemptorists there working with the immigrants, and that's how they found out about this area. One of the bishops had a brother in the neighborhood. He told them that there was a nice community growing in Chicago. So the Germans came, then the Italians. When Cabrini was built, the Italian church was destroyed, so the Italian population came into the neighborhood.

JD: When did you first come to St. Michael's?

FB: When I first came to St. Michael's in 1950, there were as many as 20 priests stationed here. From here, the Redemptorists sent missionaries throughout Illinois and into Missouri. I came again in 1960 to work with the gangs. The gypsies came in after the Italians, and to this day, the gypsy population, 80,000 concentrated around St. Alphonsus, come here to St. Michael's. There were two groups of gypsies, one from northern Europe and the other from southern Europe. This is the southern group, one that is very religious. They consider this their true parish, even though they moved north when the gangs came in.

JD: Did the gypsies live around here? We think of them as nomads.

FB: That's the group from the north. Those are the ones that have crystal balls and …are not religious at all. As a matter of fact, the two groups have nothing to do with one another. The Hungarian group are very religious. Whenever there is a wedding, baptism, or funeral, they come home to St. Michael's.

        They were the last of the ethnic groups that came in before urban renewal. Homes were knocked down, rebuilt, renovated, and so on. The gypsies couldn't stay because it became too expensive.

JD: What can you tell me about gangs in the neighborhood?

FB: I'd like to explain about the gangs. Mayor Richard J. Daley was very interested in controlling gangs. They just kept moving north until they got above North Avenue. They really took over the St. Michael's area. People would never go out. They were frightened and kept barricading themselves. I can remember many a time coming out myself and walking all the way over to the lake. I wouldn't see a soul because the people who lived here, Italians and Germans, were afraid to go out. This was in the 60's. There were five gangs all going around on the streets killing each other.

        I worked with the police going into these gangs and finding out what was going on. I tried to help them and to keep peace. Father Corbett, who was pastor of St. Michael's at the time, went out every time there was a killing to work with gang members. Although they all had their own ethnic divisions, white, black, and Puerto Rican, here in the high school, we had a lot of them all together. People in the neighborhood wouldn't send their children to the high school because they were afraid of the gangs.

What really broke up the gangs was urban renewal. When real estate companies started building and rehabbing, the gangs and their parents couldn't afford to live here any longer. They moved north where it was cheaper.

JD: Tell me about the parades St. Michael's used to hold.

FB: The parades were held on the first of April and the first of October. We wanted to encourage people to come out and honor the Virgin Mary. We carried banners and plaques through the neighborhood. Cardinal Cody told us that we were crazy and that someone was bound to get killed by the gangs. It didn't happen. As we marched around, some of the gang members took banners and joined the parade. Mayor Daley even built up the front of the church and cut off the avenue in appreciation of what the priests did with the gangs.

*Diane Gonzalez and Jane Durkott Interview Parkie Emmons,
Former Crilly Court Resident, at Her Home in Plano, Illinois, in the
Summer of 1984 (The following piece is an excerpt from the complete
interview. Since information about the Art Fair was included in the
50th Anniversary book, this has not been repeated here.)*

(Jane asks Parky about Crilly Court)

JD: Were the houses on the west side of the street single family
homes?

PE: Yes. Mr. Crilly's father had built and then sold them. His son, the
Mr. Crilly I knew, tried to get them back, but there were four he
couldn't get.

JD: Did Mr. Crilly also own the apartments that faced Crilly Court
and Wells Street?

PE: Yes, and also the Georgian Courts. Crilly Court was originally a
private street. That's why it's so short and narrow.

JD: Is that why the posts are there?

PE: Yes. Where they say Crilly Court on them. It was his father that
put them up. I don't know what his father's business was. The
family originally lived out on Prairie Avenue, I believe. There is
some debate about when the houses were built. The houses show
on a city map at the Historical Society dated 1880; so they are not
later than 1880. Architecturally, they are probably 1875 and 1880.

JD: Then, Mr. Edgar Crilly, who is the son of Daniel Crilly, also owns
the empty lot at the southeast corner of Eugenie and North Park.
And you and your neighbors got together, and he is willing to
make a park out of it, but he asks you to come up with 50 per-
cent?

PE: Well, go back one more step. The lot was originally a livery stable.
When Mr. Crilly bought it, the stable was gone, and there was
nothing but rubble.

Then came the Second World War. He turned it into Victory
Gardens and a playground for the tenants' children, which was
great. In 1948, many of us still had Victory Gardens. We'd go

down Halsted or over to the wholesale grocery district and get plants. There was a committee of tenants to run the playground and the gardens.

We decided that we needed a fence because we couldn't prevent vandalism from the neighborhood. So two of us, Martha Fish and I, went to Mr. Crilly with fear and trembling and proposed that we try to raise money for a fence if he would pay half. Mr. Crilly, who scared the daylights out of me the whole time I lived at Crilly Court, he said yes. We proposed to have a party in the back courtyard to raise the money. He wouldn't let us serve any liquor, that was his one restriction. We had square dancing, games of chance—you know where you throw things and try to hit something and you get plaster. Do you know the name plaster from carnivals? Those awful kewpie dolls. What fun! Eleanor Buhl and I were the ones who went somewhere way out on Milwaukee Avenue to buy all this plaster, and we had a grand party. And, we came up with five hundred dollars for the chain link fence.

Then the next year [1949], we repeated it to get the money for replacing play equipment, sand box, and all those things. And, of course, we invited friends from around the neighborhood. I think it was Earl Reed, although I can't be positive, who suggested that maybe an art fair on the same sort of idea would be fun.

The first meeting was, I believe, in September [1949] at Beverly's house on Lincoln. We were thinking of doing something in October, and there was a great deal of discussion about the weather being too iffy. Then it was decided that there was no way anybody could put such a thing together by October. So, it was pushed up to June [1950] the next year. Second weekend because of 57th Street…they had the first weekend.

JD: They [57th Street] must not have been juried, because all our publicity states that we are the oldest outdoor juried fair.

PE: Yes, theirs was older, but I don't think at the time that it was juried.

JD: Was Mr. Crilly still around?

PE: When did Mr. Crilly die? I don't remember. One of the reasons we moved was that he had died and then the estate was settled. They couldn't do anything with the property uneil the last trustee was gone. Then it was sold to Rubloff, and he raised the rents. We had already signed the lease and sent it back. He put the increase on over our signatures. There was nothing to be done since it was two weeks until the first of May. So we stayed for another year and thought about what else we would do?

JD: Did you move from Crilly to Plano?

PE: Yes.

JD: I have also heard that Don Herbert, Mr. Wizard, lived in the neighborhood.

PE: Don Herbert. Was he Mr. Wizard? He was that guy—the winter we had that terrible, terrible winter of 1951...where the snow was so deep no car went down Crilly Court for a week. Finally, neighbors got out and shoveled the street. And that Wizard guy—if you had shoveled yourself a parking place—he came along and stole a place consistently.

JD: You know, what we do now in the neighborhood is that everybody gets out their sawhorses or folding tables or chairs, and blocks of wood to put out when it snows. If someone takes this place, there can be real fights.

PE: Yes, well, we used to get offended if we didn't park in front of our own homes.

JD: Back to the history. Wasn't 1950 the first year for the art fair?

PE: Well, the first two years were just parties—the Crilly Court Jamborees—the ones that were held in the courtyard to raise money for the Victory Gardens. So 1950 was the first year for the Art Fair.

DG: ...Mr. Crilly used to have a painter named Babe Koenigsburg...I knew that even when rent control was established during the Second World War, Babe was kept on.

PE: Yes, Babe was the only one of three painters Mr. Crilly did keep on—really for sentimental reasons. Babe and his sister, who was mararied to Jimmy O'Toole, had grown up above Zahner's

Tavern. It belonged to their father, and I used to love to get Babe starting to talk about when the horse cars came down Wells and the farmers would come in from the truck gardens further north. They would buy feed because half of the building was tavern, and the other half was a feed store. Of course, people had horses in those days, so they had to have feed. The farmer and his family would go into the family entrance at Zahners to have their lunch or dinner.

DG: There were a number of small neighborhood stores in the Triangle, weren't there?

PE: Well, Twin Anchors, which I assume is still going strong. And then Joe Salveto's on the corner of Menomonee and Sedgwick. Is there still a bar there?

JD: That must be Marge's.

PE: Okay, she took over after Joe. He was there during prohibition, and he said he ran a very careful place. Now you could buy near-beer during that time. He had big barrels set up with two sections inside. If he knew you, he would turn the tap one way and you got real stuff; if he didn't, he turned it the other way and you got near-beer. He said he ran an orderly place. He didn't put up with no drunks or no whores. He had his bartenders trained to throw them out when they appeared.

One night, somebody in there from the neighborhood, I don't remember who it was, was making snide remarks about the Menomonee Club. Joe gave his bartenders the high sign, and they vaulted straight over the bar, grabbed this guy, and threw him out the door.

Across the street, on the northeast corner of Sedgwick and Menomonee, was a drug store. I can't remember the name of the old gentleman who ran it, but when we first moved to the Triangle, he still kept leeches and apparently sold them.

Zahner Park ran along Wells, south of Eugenie. Along Eugenie, west of the alley near Wells, there used to be an old woman who lived there. She said she wasn't running a pet shop, but the house was full of dogs and cats. The neighbors complained until finally there was a court order that she had to get rid of them. The city dogcatchers arrived to remove all of the animals. Well, Eleanor Buhl and I took our little ones, and we sat on the side steps on Eugenie across the street and watched. It was a riot! The dog-catcher would go in and come out carrying a dog. Then he would open the back door of his van to put the dog in, and two others would escape. We spent the whole morning watching them try to catch all of those animals.

JD: How was Mr. Crillly as a landlord?

PE: He was tough, but he also did very nice things. He really did. He built a baby buggy garage because of all the young women with their babies. I remember when Cathy was born, there were ten of us pregnant at the same time. The husbands complained that they couldn't get through the room at a party because of all the buggies. So, Mr. Crilly built the garage. Then, there was a family that had just such a terrible tragedy. The wife was dying of multiple sclerosis, and they had gone through everything they had or could borrow. One day, Mr. Crilly stormed into the Economy Grocery Store and demanded to see their food bill. Larry Slotkin [the owner] told Mr. Crilly, I can't show a customer's bill. Well, you didn't say no to Mr. Crilly, and he got to see it. He just said Hrumph and walked out. About 15 minutes later, his agent was back to give Dick Slotkin a check for more than the balance, which was several months in arrears. That's how he was.

The History of Old Town
through the Headlines

Lee Hill, 1990

I'm in love with Old Town. When I first came to live in Chicago, about five years ago, I would come to Old Town with my camera to photograph the architecture here, because that is what had captured my heart. Maybe that was true for many of you who decided to settle here. Physical attraction is usually the first step in a love affair.

But, over time, I've come to know more about this community's past. I've seen it during difficult times— like when its residents were torn apart over the Eugenie high-rise controversy—and I've seen Old town in joyous times, like its very successful art fairs.

I've come to know many of Old Town's residents as people. I've felt the spirit here that has helped this special neighborhood endure over the years. I celebrate its uniqueness. For me, love at first sight has grown to a deeper kind of devotion.

Reporters serve another role than just bringing the news. They are outside observers, not caught up in what they are covering as journalists. So when they report events, it's from a more detached perspective than those who are living through them. By examining how reporters have written about Old Town over the decades, a new perspective can be gained.

Old Town started out as a cabbage patch doll. That's right. In the early 1840's it was basically a truck farm for Chicago, producing celery, potatoes, and cabbages. It was called the Cabbage Patch long before it gained the more respectable name of North Town. It's only been called Old Town for about the past 50 years.

It was a farming community back then, for the German settlement around Chicago Avenue west of what is now called Clark Street— the old St. Joseph's parish. Some from that parish eventually moved up here from the city, including Michael Diversey and the Wackers. But in the late 1940s, a new wave of German immigrants moved into the area. They called themselves the '48ers. Dagmar Harper, a docent with the Chicago Historical Society who helped organize that group's tours of Old Town about 10 years ago, wrote This new wave of immigrants was the intelligentsia—people who sought freedom of thought, and so they left Germany and settled here. They were largely professionals: educators, artists, and writers. You might say, it was Old Town's first wave of yuppies.

It was this group, along with the financial help of Michael Diversey, who scraped together the $730 it took to build St. Michael's Church in 1852. Two years later, they added a school. It was Father John Mueller of St. Michael's who first whipped this community together, fostering a cohesive spirit that is found here today.

These first immigrants were joined by the Scotch, Hungarians, Italians, Irish, Assyrians, Filipinos, Greeks, Japanese, you name it. That type of diversity has always been a hallmark of Old Town. One Tribune article, written by Norma Lee Browning in 1957, noted that one of the community's potluck dinners once featured dishes from 28 nationalities. And Amy and Maurice Forkert told me that often people attending potluck dinners in later years could not communicate in the same language, so they dug out their musical instruments and communicated that way.

It was a good thing that a community spirit had developed back then, because nearly everyone's home was destroyed in the Chicago Fire in October 1871. It was not going to be the last time Chicago had to deal with its homeless.

St. Michael's, too, was destroyed. During the fire, people gathered in the street and watched the church and school they had worked so hard to build just disintegrate in the flames. But when the fire died down, Old Towners gathered up shovels and brooms and began to clear the debris. A year and three days later, St. Michael's was restored.

And so, North Town continued to grow, as did post-fire Chicago. Now that a bridge had been built over the Chicago River, more and more newcomers poured into what is now Old Town. And, like it has throughout its history, the old welcomed the new.

The city was vibrant and alive. Win Stracke wrote a piece for the Chicago Tribune magazine nearly 20 years ago, recalling what Old Town was like during his childhood, around 1910-1911.

"The old neighborhood was noisy as hell," he recalled. "The Halsted Street cars rattled along without benefit of wheel bearings... the elevated was then used at more than capacity with the screeching of local express trains going around the triple curve at North Avenue and Halsted...

My young ears were filled with the sound of wagons: ash wagons, garbage wagons, grocery wagons, moving wagons, clanging paddy wagons, Brink's wagons, brewery wagons, junk wagons, sprinkler wagons, department store wagons, popcorn wagons, and lumber wagons.

There were delightful summertime visits of the waffle wagon—a white, glass-enclosed conveyance drawn by one horse, from which a Greek man sold his rectangular waffles, dusted with sugar, fresh from the gridiron.

There was Andy Laflin, who came around with a wagon selling only two products, kerosene and vinegar. At this distance in time, his combination of products seems a little strange. Maybe the vinegar was a hedge against the dwindling kerosene business due to the increasingly widespread use of gas for lighting. Anyway, Andy Laflin was trying to survive in a neighborhood which had rejected him as the Socialist candidate for alderman—an office he had lost to Paddy Bauler's older brother, Herman."

Old Towners were a lively set. Over on Crilly Court, Essanay Studio tycoon George K. Spoor kept things hopping. As Virginia Lee wrote in the Chicago American in 1963, Spoor kept film in his icebox and held swinging parties in the Court for his stars: Bronco Billy Anderson, Francis X Bushman and his leading lady-wife Beverly Bayne, Gloria Swanson and her first husband Wallace Beery…Spoor further enlivened the neighborhood by staging his first Keystone Kop chase down Eugenie Street and through the Court.

Nor was that to be the last of Old Town's picture-making days. In 1986, Jack and Mike, a television series, was back on Crilly Court, Wells Street, and North Avenue to shoot for Gerber-MGM Pictures.

George Murray of the Chicago American wrote in 1957 that in the early '20's, the art quarter was centered around the Dill Pickle Club in Tooker Alley. Ben Hecht and Charlie MacArthur took a studio at 1839 Lincoln Park West, near other painters, sculptors, composers and poets who had talent and taste.

Then, with the Great Depression, hard times hit Old Town, as it did everywhere. To make ends meet, many of the older, large homes were broken up into smaller, more affordable living spaces. Albert Jedlicka Jr. of the Chicago Daily News wrote this about Old Town: a fashionable center of town houses in the gas light era, Old Town had degenerated into a section of flea-bag rooming houses by the 1940s.

It was in the 1930s that an influx of artistic types began—a trend that would continue for the next 20-30 years. Musicians, artists, writers, theater, radio, and film people were drawn to this neighborhood, once again filling it with diversity.

It became what Sheri Blair described as Chicago's answer to the Left Bank. She wrote that Old Town had become home to Henry Rago, editor of Poetry Magazine; to writer Herman Kogan; to Paul Angle of the Historical Society; to cartoonist Bill Mauldin; even to ex-boxer Max Marek who came here to open a bookstore.

To that list, Marge Lyon of the Chicago Tribune, added Francis Chapin and TV's Mr. Wizard. And she makes note of a key characteristic about the interesting, creative people who populated the Old Town neighborhood, one that I think still thrives today. She wrote, "In the Triangle, the Smiths do not try to keep up with the Joneses. Both the Smiths and the Joneses are busy keeping up with their own clever ideas. One of my favorite Old Towners, Edgar Miller, came here to live and work and to transform some homes under his skilled artistic hand."

Many other very artistic and energetic people migrated here in the late 30s and early 40s—among them Lyle Mayer, who recalled that when he moved here in 1936, there already were a few hardy souls beginning to improve things in the neighborhood.

Indeed, the 1940s and 1950s were a whirlwind of saws, hammers, and paintbrushes in Old Town. Albert Jedlicka Jr. wrote that James Beverly, a business engineer and chief librarian for a judge, bought three adjoining buildings around 1946 for $14,500, and then spent nearly $66,000 renovating the structures. Similarly, he reported Ed Kunkel bought a four-story rooming house for $20,000 and spent another $40,000 in renovations. He then was able to charge rents ranging from $88.50 for the smallest apartment to $210 for a two-level, four-bedroom unit.

About this time, Old Towners were very proud of what they had wrought in this neighborhood. As a way of celebrating their own creativity and of showing off this beautiful neighborhood, the Triangle held "open house"—what then was called the Old Town Holiday and what was to become known as the annual Old Town Art Fair.

George Murray of the Chicago American wrote that each spring, it became a crick-in-the-back time—everyone spent evenings and weekends toiling like slave laborers—digging, planting, raking, rolling, designing, building, painting…for the strollers.

Was it any wonder then, as more and more outsiders—strollers, if you will, who came by the art fair and fell in love with the area's ambiance, the creativity, the energy of Old Town, was it any surprise, then, that they would be attracted to the neighborhood? Of course, some saw Old Town's quaintness as a way to make money.

And thus, Wells Street was reborn — not in the quiet, classy way the residential district had been rehabbed, but in a garish jangle of simulated quasi-quaintness that became Wells Street in the 1960s.

Writer Joan Kufrin told how she woke one day to find her beloved Old Town changed almost overnight. She wrote this in the Chicago Daily News: "A once quiet patch of land known as Old Town to its devoted residents, who had labored long and hard to preserve its distinct atmosphere, suddenly was overtaken by a contagious, creeping senility. At first, it was an elusive phenomenon. One merely noticed a growing number of antique shops- — any, many antique shops. Then, abruptly, an old building on Wells Street was given a reverse face lifting, at great cost, to make it appear even older than it was. And a neighboring building, as though ashamed of its comparative youth, went through the same eerie aging process.

Into one newly aged building went an old-time saloon with brass rails and spittoons. Into another, a 1903 ice cream parlor with old-fashioned sundaes. An automatic laundry closed one evening and was reborn the next day as a penny-candy store. A garage evicted its automobiles and became an authentic general store with bins of dry goods, a baroque cash register, and bewhiskered and beaproned help."

As Kufrin put it, the new had to make way for the old. She recalls the Grey Line buses bringing out-of-towners here — 4-H clubs from Kankakee, Women's Clubs from Peoria and Peotone, Elks, Moose, and Shriners from everywhere…

Why? Why this incredible magnetism to such quasi-quaintness? Who better to answer that question than Slim Brundage, the creator of the College of Complexes, an establishment that flourished here and was reincarnated a couple of times. In 1965, Brundage wrote in an article for the Chicago Tribune: "Last week, I met John Moody. He's the cat who really made Wells Street swing when he opened Moody's Pub in November 1960 at 1529 North Wells. When they tripled his rent, he moved to 1800 North Larrabee and is still swinging there.

Anyway, he came up with the usual question: What has Wells Street got going for it? That made me think about it. What does a street really have to have? Why, COLOR! And this is the street that's got more of that stuff than any other street in America."

Although, technically, Wells Street is not part of the Old Town Triangle, it was the success, the rich diversity of this residential district that spawned the growth and success of Wells Street. It was the interesting people here that drew others who wanted to be a part of that feeling.

Joan Kufrin wrote, "For there flourished in Old Town an exciting, exotic type of social life. With everyone dressed for fun and games, no one could tell who or what anyone was. A bank president might break pretzels with a beatnik; a poet brush knees with a Winnetka housewife; and no one knew the difference. It marked the beginning of the classless society."

Anonymous one and all, we drank together, ankle-deep in peanut shells and sawdust, crowded at miniscule, aging tables, and seated on splintered, desiccated wooden chairs. Served by deft waitresses who could lug four steins in each hand, we toasted Old Town for its four-dollar hamburgers and one-dollar sundaes.

Ah, but once again, Old Town's boom times came to bust. The Tribune's Paul Gapp wrote With the boom of the 1960s came two changes. The first was an influx of hippies, pseudo-hippies, bikers, freaks, and runaway kids looking for a place to crash. The second change was increased commercial rent, which drove out some amateur entrepreneurs.

Indeed, with Wells Street's wild success, rents had quadrupled in five years to where one restaurant, renting on a percentage basis, was paying $2,780 a month. Residential prices soared too. Fred Henry, then president of the Old Town Triangle Association, was asked by Gilbert Jiminez of the Sun Times to evaluate Chicago's Haight-Asbury days.

It's got good points and bad points, Henry noted. Maybe the neighborhood is a little bit more stable, but we've probably driven out some of the more creative people—people that might depend upon low rents and small apartments.

The Chicago American's Dorothy Collins, in an article entitled "Will Success Spoil Old Town?" brought up many points about Old Town's success—points that are still valid today. She wrote in 1965: "Old Town, Chicago's never-never land of instant quaintness, may be killing itself with success…not that Old Town is going to fold its movie-set store fronts and creep into bankruptcy statistics. But it has expanded too quickly, gotten too cute, and been invaded by those in search of the fast buck."

Writer Greg Ramshaw wrote in 1969 about vacant storefronts now dotting the once-clogged Wells Street. He quoted Harold Milner, part owner of the Emporium: "Some keep their rents so high that only bars and restaurants can make it—and even they have a high turnover."

In a 1967 article by Donna Gill in the Chicago Tribune, she quotes urban renewal manager George Stone: "The whole thing might get too rich for our blood. That is a danger. The area might be limited only to professionals."

In the 1960s, people who love this area worried about it becoming so successful that it would displace all but the upper class, and thereby lose the diversity that has given Old Town its special flavor and flair over the decades. I suppose that is a legitimate fear—one which I wonder about from time to time as I cover events here. I won't try to predict Old Town's future—what will become of this unique neighborhood. But I will tell you this: I believe in Old Town. I think it will survive any passing threat to its liveliness.

From the earliest times to today, I think people will continue to fall in love with Old Town and will fight to keep it something special. Because the people here are special. It's not just architecture that makes this historic district so unique. It never has been just that. The buildings here have been built and burned, rebuilt, and rehabbed. They've gone from bedraggled to bedecked. What HAS endured is the spirit of this community. The spirit of the people here who rebuilt St. Michael's in one year—the creativity of the people here who see beneath shabby shingles—the cohesiveness of the people here who can fight vigorously about a high rise and then mend the temporary divisiveness it caused.

Old Town's future—like its past—is very, very rich.

My Old Town

DAN BALDWIN, 2001

Dan Baldwin is an Old Town resident and its most avid promoter. He has served as an OTTA board member, President of the Board, art fair Security Chair, and Historic District Committee Chair.

I have lived in Old Town for more than 15 years…which is like stopping by for a cup of coffee compared to the tenure of most of my friends and neighbors. Though I was single when I moved here, I met my wife Lucy in Old Town, had two children here, raised one dog, and am now on the second. We have lived on Clark, Orleans, Lincoln, North Park, Crilly Court, and Lincoln Park West—twice.

We enjoy the positive things this neighborhood has to offer: the convenience to the Loop (I am a bicycle commuter year-round), the Zoo, North Avenue beach (we swim summer evenings at the chess pavilion), Lincoln Park for dog walks (yes, we pick up after him), the Historical Society, and the many convenient restaurants and stores—especially John's market, where they still have house charge accounts.

It's nice to have local options for shopping. At one time, the Triangle was all small specialty stores. Every year, more seem to throw in the towel, unable to compete with the big box category killers on Clybourn. It's great to see Tipre Hardware survive in the area, even when Sears moved in across the street. (Sears lasted six months.)

The Old Town Triangle is clearly a unique area of Chicago. With its specifically defined boundaries—Clark, Ogden, North—we are able to maintain and continue a kind of brand name recognition, not diluted by Real Estate brochures. Currently, these brochures advise that you can buy an [overpriced] Lincoln Park condo on the corner of Ashland and Wellington. If you read of an affordable place listed as Old Town, it's probably on Division and Larrabee, in the area formerly known as Cabrini Green.

Most of the major construction changes to the neighborhood occurred before I moved in, and although we did protest Eugenie Towers, working to save a vacant lot was not as romantic as saving an historic building from the wrecking ball. We are very fortunate for the work done to create the Landmark District. Without it, half the homes in the

Triangle, including my own, would be gone in a year to make room for more monster houses that appear to be looking for a golf course.

In some respects, I think it's the neighborhood character and design and its commitment to the preservation of that character that keeps the culture intact. People come and go, but the neighborhood endures. Many of the people who come are actually content to live with the limited space that gracious older homes offer and will suffer parking restrictions in order to sit on their porches chatting with neighbors on warm summer evenings. They accept that historic can mean slightly shabby, a little leaky, maybe no air conditioning, and are even willing to shovel the roof when it snows—you read that right, the roof. Contrast this with other areas where houses sit on two lots, and residents rush into garages with breezeways that afford them a coatless commute to work. Yet, these people are probably not lucky enough to have neighbors who come out to help them sweep the alley in the spring, or water the trees on the parkway.

And, speaking of the parkways, I want to stress the beauty of the trees in the Triangle. If you look at old photos of the neighborhood, you will see how small the trees are compared with those we have today. That's because the Old Town Triangle Association has done a great job of keeping a tree in every well. I would venture to say that when our crabapples are blooming, they rival the cherry blossoms in Washington, D.C., and it isn't easy keeping trees healthy with our Chicago winters. We have lost nearly all of our giant cottonwoods, but we have planted more than 20 trees a year since I have been here. The trees are nearly as historic as the buildings.

I remember when we went door to door on Eugenie Street explaining that the trees would be trimmed so that the city could do new sewer work. One resident was so upset that her tree, which is about 50 feet tall, would be ruined. She had planted the tree the day her son went off to fight in the Second World War. Our trees, like our houses, have great stories attached to them. As for me, when I walk around the neighborhood, I can remember and point out every tree that I helped plant, water, or order from the city. How many people in other city neighborhoods can say that?

Old Town: A Moveable Feast

BY RICK GREENWOOD,
President Old Town Triangle Association, 2000-2001

If only Hemingway had not lived in Paris during his most productive writing years, I could sum up my feelings about how I (and many of my neighbors) feel about Old Town without resorting to plagiarism. You see, those of us who live here really do feel that our neighborhood is A Moveable Feast.

To explain how I feel about Old Town, I'm going to ask you to put your car keys in your pocket and take a walk with me. We'll start by crossing Clark Street and walking through the Chicago Historical Society; a magnificent institution dedicated to preserving our City's history—right here where we live. We come out on one of the most beautiful and historically interesting parks in the city—our own Lincoln Park, home of a world class zoo and a host of famous statues. You can check them out. Further east, Lake Michigan, one of the world's largest inland lakes, fills us with awe and appreciation for both its size and beauty.

Since man (and woman) does not live by beauty alone, we haven't far to go to satisfy our stomachs, as well as our senses. If we crave Chicago's best (arguably) ribs and a noisy neighborhood atmosphere, we head to Twin Anchors at Eugenie and Sedgwick. If it's haute cuisine we want, Charlie Trotter's, a short walk north on Armitage, is ranked as one of the finest restaurants in the world. In between we have Bistrot Margot, Kamehachi, Old Jerusalem, and Topo Gigio on Wells, Dinotto's on North Avenue, and I could go on. As for nightlife, Zanie's tickles our funny bone, Park West fills our ears with music, and Second City challenges our imagination.

But we aren't through yet. As we continue our walk, it becomes even more evident that Old Town has it all. We have excellent schools: Lincoln Elementary, the Latin School, the LaSalle Language Academy, and Lincoln Park High School; and we have access to incomparable health care—Northwestern Memorial Hospital and Children's Memorial Hospital. We keep walking past landmark buildings, dry cleaners, florists, coffee shops, pharmacies, bookstores, groceries, bakers, movie theaters, someone stop me, please.

All this, and we still haven't seen the best of Old Town. To truly understand what makes this part of Chicago special, you have to get to know the people who live here. And the more time you spend with us, the better you can appreciate how our neighborhood and our neighbors are such an important part of our lives. So much so, that, like Hemingway, wherever we go in this world, we take Old Town with us. Because, our Old Town is A Moveable Feast.

CHAPTER 16

TO INFINITY AND BEYOND:
A Few Who Made a Difference

> *Andy Warhol once said that everyone could be famous for 15 min-*
> *utes. Maybe that was his way of saying fame is fleeting. I don't*
> *know. I do know that, through the years, we have had neighbors*
> *who will be famous far longer than a quarter of an hour—perhaps*
> *even to infinity and beyond, to quote the children's action hero*
> *Buzz Lightyear. Here are just a few of Old Town's sons and daugh-*
> *ters whose achievements have made life better and more beautiful*
> *for all of us. Some are no longer with us; others we are still privi-*
> *leged to call neighbor. To all of them, we say, thank you.*

(* Indicates deceased)

IVAN ALBRIGHT,* loyal Triangle member who died in 1983, was one of the most important artists of the 20th century, known for his unique painting style. His main theme was the deterioration of human beings with age. One of his most famous paintings, entitled *That which I should have done, I did not do*, shows a wrinkled hand closing an ancient door decorated with a wreath and a faded rose. He also painted *The Picture of Dorian Grey*.

PAUL ANGLE* was a renowned Lincoln scholar and Director of the Chicago Historical Society. He lived in the Triangle for nearly 30 years and, with his wife and daughter, Paula, worked tirelessly for the community, especially the Art Fair. The photograph all of us who live in Old Town have etched in our memories is that of Paul

HOME OF PAUL ANGLE, MENOMONEE AND LINCOLN PARK WEST

in his robe, looking benignly at the paintings hanging on his fence during the first Old Town Holiday in 1950.

DR. HENRY BETTS, longtime neighbor and Triangle member, is Chair of the Rehabilitation Institute Foundation in Chicago. His contributions to the field of rehabilitation medicine and his efforts to improve the lives of others have brought him worldwide recognition. Recently, Ohio State University bestowed its highest honor upon him: the Honorary Degree, Doctor of Public Service.

FRANCIS CHAPIN.* Collectors sought him out, colleges and universities vied for his services as a visiting professor, and exhibitors clamored for his work. His paintings were shown in museums all over the world, yet he never failed to show his work at his beloved Old Town Art Fair. Admirers bequeathed him lofty titles, his neighbors simply called him Chape, and acknowledged that he was one of America's best loved artists and creative colorists.

DANIEL CRILLY* was a south side real estate developer when he bought a large tract of land bounded by Wells Street, North Park, Eugenie, and St. Paul in 1884. He cut a one-block street through the middle of the property and called it Crilly Court. In 1885, he built 12 row houses on the west side of the street with materials purchased from Germania Place. The houses were used as rental properties for middle class professionals who were moving into the neighborhood. He then moved three buildings from Germania Place to 1717-1719 N. North Park and had three apartment buildings designed by Flanders and Zimmerman built at 1701-1713 N. North Park. In 1888, Crilly commissioned Flanders and Zimmerman to design the commercial and apartment buildings from 1700 to 1718 N. Wells Street. These buildings are used as a model for one Chicago building type by the Chicago Landmarks Commission. In 1895, the four apartment buildings on the east side of Crilly Court were built, each with the name of one of Crilly's children carved above the doorway: Isabelle, Oliver, Erminnie, and Edgar.

RONA TALCOTT DAVIS. Most people know Rona as the foremost Old Town cheerleader and owner of the magnificent four-story house on the corner of North Park and Menomonee. They also recognize her as an incomparable hostess at art fair time. What they may not know is that, as Rona Talcott, she is an internationally renowned photographer who is constantly being summoned to distant parts of the world to record people, places, and events for posterity.

MICHAEL DIVERSEY* (1810-1869) came to Chicago from Germany in 1841. He was a partner in the prosperous Lill and Diversey Brewery, located at the corner of Chicago and Pine Street (Michigan Avenue). Throughout his life, Diversey supported the German community in North Town. He donated land at the corner of North Avenue and Church Street (Hudson) to build a church for German farmers living in the Cabbage Patch (Old Town). The church was dedicated to St. Michael, his patron saint. He also sold much of his land to enable the City of Chicago to extend its northern boundary to Fullerton Street, encouraging many of the city's most prominent citizens to move into the area.

HERMAN KOGAN* was one of Chicago's most prolific and respected writers. Kogan worked for every newspaper in the city before becoming editor of the *Chicago Sun Times*. With Lloyd Wendt, he co-authored a number of books about Chicago biographies of notorious politicians John "Bathhouse" Coughlin and Michael "Hinky

Dink" Kenna. Perhaps his best known effort was the history of Marshall Field, & Co., *Give the Lady What She Wants.*

SOL KOGEN AND EDGAR MILLER* met at the School of the Art Institute in 1917. Kogen was an entrepreneur and artist who worked in his family's dry goods business before moving to Paris. Miller was raised in Idaho where he was influenced by Native American artists. When Kogen returned to Chicago in 1927, he invited Miller to help him reinvent West Burton Place (then called Carl Street). They used the street's old flats and tenements as an urban canvas and established Old Town as an artists' community. They redecorated the old Victorian houses using a freehand Art Deco style. Some, they merely embellished. Others got brick facades and

ICHi-17834, Photographer unknown

THE KOGEN MILLER STUDIO AT 1734 N. WELLS.

new additions. They didn't bother with building permits, and rarely consulted architects. Kogen and Miller scavenged Maxwell Street for tiles, copper tubs, wooden doors, and hardware. Since their funds were limited, they worked on one apartment at a time. When one was finished, it was rented to get money for the next conversion. Some were never finished. Like Topsy, they grew and grew and grew. In 1928, Kogen and Miller began remodeling a studio at 1734 N. Wells. With very little documentation, they built onto the front, raised the building, and put on a top addition. Today, the carved doors and windows, stained glass, decorative plaques, and ceramic tiles from their scavenged collection are among Old Town's treasures.

RICHARD LATHAM.* When Mande Latham was a little girl, her classmates asked her what her father did for a living. She went home and posed that question to her dad. You go back to school tomorrow, he answered, and tell them to walk around their houses. Look in the kitchen drawers, open the cabinets, pass by the refrigerator, and look inside. I designed something that is in every one of them. Indeed he did design refrigerators, cabinetry, and all sorts of kitchen utensils for the Ecco company: spatulas, spoons, egg beaters, and knives. He designed the red, white, and blue logo for the (then) Standard Oil Company. He even designed the smokestack for the Queen Mary. Many of you might find Rosenthal porcelain in your cabinets imprinted with the inscription A.G. Form 2000. The pattern was Dick's design. His dinnerware is in the permanent collection of the Museum of Modern Art in New York. The sailing world called Richard Latham its own. President of the United States Yacht Racing Union, he won the coveted Herreshoff Trophy in 1982. He also helped organize America's Cup competitions and the sailing feature of the Olympic Games. Crediting his wife Mary Ann for "making me who I am," Dick believed in giving back to the society that supported him and endowed a foundation at IIT to help young designers. He was also a very practical and unassuming man. Asked about his theory of design he replied, *Chicago is a horse collar town. Design is there to pull a wagon, not decorate a horse.*

DAWN CLARK NETSCH has served her neighborhood, her state, and her nation with great distinction. As delegate to the Illinois Constitutional Convention in 1970, Dawn was vice-chair of the Revenue and Finance Committee and played a major role in writing our state's Constitution. She represented Chicago's Fourth Legislative District in the Illinois State Legislature from 1973 to 1991 as Chairman of the Senate Revenue Committee and Co-chair of the Illinois Economic and Fiscal Commission. Dawn was the first woman to be elected to a state constitutional executive office, the Office of Comptroller in 1990. She was a formidable candidate for state governor in 1994. Currently, she teaches law at Northwestern University. She has been honored for her accomplishments in government by Common Cause, the Illinois Environmental Council, the Illinois Humanities Council, the Illinois Alcoholism and Drug Dependence Association, the Illinois Public Action Council, the Illinois Education Association and the YWCA. She was also the first recipient of the First Annual

United States Supreme Court Justice John Paul Stevens Award and the Federal District Court and Federal Bar Association Award for Excellence in Pro Bono Service. Old Town residents and guests recognize Dawn from the art fair auction where, for a number of years she has helped raise money for the Triangle Association as a celebrity auctioneer.

WALTER NETSCH. An architect and designer of great talent and versatility, Walter studied at MIT. He first practiced in the Chicago suburbs, then joined the firm of Skidmore, Owings, & Merrill (SOM) where he developed an innovative architectural style which he called "field theory." His projects include the Astronomical Research Center, Administration Building, and the libraries at Northwestern University; the Library, Student Center, and Pavilion at the University of Illinois Chicago (UIC); the U. S. Air Force Academy in Colorado Springs; the Skokie Public Library; St. Matthew's Methodist Church, Evanston; and the East Wing of the Art Institute of Chicago. A past president of the Park District's Board of Commissioners Walter established a five-year plan that included new design and construction of 100 children's playlots each year. He also created a department of research and planning and worked with architects and planners to improve the quality of park design.

HADDON SUNBLOOM.* For many years Sunbloom lived in one of the Crilly apartments above the Wells Street stores. While not many may have heard of

COCA COLA SANTA
BY HADDON SUNBLOOLM.

Photo courtesy of the Coca Cola Company

the man, everyone recognizes his work. He created the kindly man on the Quaker Oats box and Aunt Jemima. His Coca-Cola Santa is still an annual Christmas feature all over the world.

CHARLES H. WACKER* was born in 1856 and made his fortune in the brewing business. He was a great civic leader, who, like the current Mayor Richard M. Daley, led a movement to beautify Chicago's lakefront and to improve traffic conditions in the city by widening the major north/south streets leading to the downtown business area. He also proposed moving the South Water Market from the south branch of the Chicago River and replacing it with a modern double-decker thoroughfare. That thoroughfare now bears his name. Wacker was president of the Chicago Relief and Aid Society and the United Charities of Chicago. He was also director of the Chicago Chapter of the American Red Cross. True to his Old Town German, he had a strong influence on German-American activities in the city, acting as treasurer of the German Opera House Company, director of the German Old People's Home, and a member of several German singing societies. His childhood home at 1838 N. Lincoln Park West is an architectural landmark in the Old Town Triangle.

HARRY WEESE.* His wife Kitty said it best—Harry Weese's creations were models of intelligence. His office buildings, auditoriums, city halls, schools, libraries, and even the metropolitan transit system for Washington, D.C., are uncommonly cordial and gracious. His houses are small, inviting, and filled with fun. Think of witty roofs and entries, improbable but logical windows, and suddenly opened spaces, and you cannot help but remember the brilliance that was Harry Weese. He loved the city and saw Chicago as a stimulus to fresh thought about how people could and should live. Like Daniel Burnham, he was a city planner and developed a number of five-year plans for improving life in Our Town. He rejected orthodoxy, opting instead for freedom of design, lightness of mood, and structural economy. Both his residential and non-residential works welcome people to enter and enjoy—from the lobby of the Time-Life Building, to the building at 200 South Wacker Drive. And who but Weese could design a high-security federal prison in a compassionate way? The jail just south of Chicago's Loop is triangular shaped with open cell areas that resemble the common rooms of his University of Chicago dormitories. His finest houses were prototypes for what could be done on reasonable budgets. His row house on Willow Street in the Old Town Triangle, was designed as part of a private urban renewal four-townhouse plan. Others in the row are similar, but each reflects the owner's needs and desires. The house that he and Kitty shared manages to be typically Old Town and even more typically Harry: small scale, light, gracious, whimsical, and welcoming. The neighborhood, the city, the nation, and the world are better places because of Harry Weese.

KITTY WEESE. When most of us think of Kitty, we see her magnificent water color paintings. But Kitty the artist is only the latest reincarnation of a brilliant and talented woman. She graduated with a degree in child psychology from the University of London and practiced first in the Children's Clinic in Richmond, Virginia, and later in Montgomery, Alabama. Her brother, Ben Baldwin, was an architect who studied city planning under Eliel Saarinen at the Cranbrook Academy of Art in Michigan. It was there he met Harry Weese whom he introduced to his sister, and as Kitty said, arranged the marriage. It would be easy to say the rest is history—but that is far from the truth. With Harry's encouragement, Kitty went into partnership with Jody Kingrey and, in 1947, they opened the Baldwin Kingrey Good Design Store, importing modern furniture and household effects from Scandinavia. She also opened the first art gallery in Chicago that same year. She sold the store to raise her children, but when the fledglings could fly on their own, Kitty also took flight. She went into interior design and did the interiors of many buildings designed by her husband, including three floors of the Sears Tower. Still, this amazing woman's creativity was not satisfied. She had yet another career waiting in the wings. She became interested in painting and studied botanical illustration at the Botanic Gardens. She also took courses in Aspen, Colorado. Bolstered by both her instructors, she started painting more and found her way to the Old Town Art Center where she still paints. Kitty's botanicals have become famous throughout the city and in Colorado where she has had a number of one-woman shows. She recently exhibited her works with fellow artists John Holabird and Norman Zimmerman at the

Old Town Art Gallery. From her town house on Willow Street, Kitty sings the praises of the Triangle, calling it a wonderful neighborhood. We agree.

JOHNNY WEISMULLER.* Often called the greatest swimmer of the 20th century, Johnny grew up at 1921 North Cleveland Avenue and was an altar boy at St. Michael's Church. He was one of many children who got free cookies from the Pipers when he went into their bakery on Wells Street. He set world records at the 1924 Olympics in Paris in both the 100- and 400-meter free style events and won the 100-meter race in Amsterdam four years later. Weismuller is perhaps best known for his portrayal of Tarzan in the movies and Jungle Jim.

The Old Town Triangle Association — A Chronology

1945   A group of Old Town neighbors decided to form a club to provide city children with wholesome recreation. With the help of Joe Vitale, Executive Director of the North Side Boys Clubs, they rented an Old Town storefront and began offering afternoon and evening activities, such as baseball, football, boxing, tumbling, Ping-Pong, shuffleboard, woodcraft, and choral singing. With membership a mere 50 cents a year, more than 100 children had joined within a few weeks. Five years later, the club found a permanent home at 244 West Willow in a former bowling alley. It is still there and is now called The Menomonee Club for Boys and Girls.

1948   The first town meeting was held to establish the Old Town Triangle Association. Its formation came about as a result of promotional efforts by the North Side Planning Council under the leadership of Earl H. Reed. The Triangle, which took its name from the large three-sided area formed by the junction of Clark Street, North Avenue, and Ogden Avenue, promised to preserve the charm of the Old Town Triangle and to promote improved living, shopping, working, and recreational facilities.

1949   The Triangle Association and the LaSalle School Parent/Teachers Association planted trees in the parkways and drew up an ambitious program of objectives which included (1) improving traffic

control, (2) installing better garbage containers and pest elimina-
tion, (3) supervising zoning enforcement, and (4) encouraging
lending agencies to support residential improvements. The organization was also to serve as a forum for all matters affecting the
neighborhood, especially building preservation and youth activities. James Beverly became the Association's first President.

1952   The Old Town Triangle Association incorporated and registered
with the State of Illinois. The Articles of Incorporation noted that
the purpose of the Association was to improve the conditions of
life, work, recreation, health and safety of the neighborhood. The
organization pledged to foster and develop a neighborhood plan
and to aid, assist, and sponsor neighborhood activities in the area
bounded by Ogden Avenue, North Avenue, and Clark Street.

1956   The Old Town Art Center was established by the Triangle
Association to serve as a gallery and art workshop. Neighbors
hoped that the Center would enhance appreciation of the visual
arts in the community through exhibits, lectures, and art classes.

1964   The Association received a 501-(c) (4) designation. In 1982, the
Internal Revenue Service changed this designation to 501-(c) (3).

1965   The neighborhood agreed to become Project I of the Lincoln
Park General Neighborhood Renewal Plan under the aegis of the
United States Department of Urban Renewal.

1967-72 The Historic American Buildings Survey and the Illinois Historic
Structures Survey resulted in many Old Town buildings being
placed on the permanent list in the Department of Conservation
in Springfield and the Library of Congress in Washington.

1977   Through the efforts of Association Directors and concerned community members, the Old Town Triangle District was designated
an Historical Chicago Landmark by the City Council of Chicago
on September 28, 1977.

1983   The Old Town Triangle Association (OTTA) moved to its present
location at 1763 N. North Park Avenue, at the other end of the
block from the Menomonee Club. In this new, more spacious
site, the Association was able to expand its community activities
and continue its ongoing art classes and gallery exhibitions.

APPENDIX B

Presidents,
Old Town Triangle Association

1948-50	James E. Beverly	1984	Fred Henry
1951-52	Robert M. Switzer, Jr.	1985-86	Betty Fromm
1953-55	Pierre Blouke	1987-88	Bruno Ast
1956-57	Bertram Murray	1989-90	Monika Betts
1958-59	John A. Cook	1991-92	Roger Skolnik
1960-61	David M. Landis	1993-95	Shirley Baugher
1962-63	Roy Russinof	1996-97	Dan Baldwin
1964	Lucille Hecht	1998-99	Scott Early
1965	Mrs. Pierre Blouke	2000-01	Rick Greenwood
1966-67	Thomas C. Eley		
1968-69	Mrs. O. M. Forkert		
1970-71	James G. Donegan		
1972-73	Alan Rappaport		
1974	Robert A. Davidson		
1975	Edward L. Klinenberg		
1976-77	Maurice Forkert		
1978	Carol Graham		
1979	Paul Kuhn		
1980-81	Elizabeth Barnhill		
1982	Larry Blust		
1983	Hannah Sue Samuels		

Officers and Directors, Old Town Triangle Association

Please note, the names appear as they were recorded in the Minutes by the respective secretaries. In some instances, no first names were given. There is no archival information for the years 1955-1962 and 1968.

1951
President Robert Switzer, Jr.
1st Vice President Frederick W. Gotham
2nd Vice President Monica Surgott
Secretary Joan Ransom
Treasurer Mr. Dean
Directors James Beverly, Pierre Blouke, Monica Surgott

1952-53
President Pierre Blouke
1st Vice President Monica Surgott
2nd Vice President Bert Murray
Secretary/Treasurer Mary Van Nortwick
Directors James Beverly, Jeanette McDaniel, Eugene Sullivan, Miss Campbell, John Cook

1954

President Pierre Blouke
1st Vice President Bert Murray
2nd Vice President John Cook
Secretary Mrs. Roger Ingalls
Treasurer Eleanor Clement
Director Mrs. Paul Angle
Director Mrs. Paul Hay

1962

President Roy Russinof
1st Vice President William G. Hyer
2nd Vice President Olin Neill
Emmons
Secretary Helena Clayton
Treasurer Victoria S. MacDonald
Directors Mrs. Pierre Blouke, Todd
A. Ebbers, Dr. Robert R. J.
Hilker, Harry D. Lavery,
Bert Ray, Sarajane Wells

1963

President Roy M. Russinof
1st Vice President William G. T. Hyer
2nd Vice President Olin Neill
Emmons
Secretary Helena Clayton
Treasurer Victoria S. MacDonald
Directors Franz Altschuler, Mrs.
Pierre Blouke, Dr. Robert
R. J. Hilker, Very Rev. H.
J. Novak, CSSR, Bert Ray,
Sarajane Wells

1964

President Mrs. Pierre Blouke
1st Vice President Dr. Robert R. J.
Hilker
2nd Vice President Paul M. Angle
Secretary Mrs. Samuel J. Palormo
Treasurer David L. Soltker
Directors Thomas C. Eley, Jack
Ringer

1965

President Lucille Hecht
1st Vice President Dr. Robert R. J.
Hilker
2nd Vice President Daniel Marcus
Secretary Helena Clayton
Treasurer David L. Soltker
Directors Franz Altschuler, Mrs.
Pierre Blouke, Thomas C.
Eley, Mrs. Robert Nickle,
Very Rev. H. J.
Novak,CSSR, Richard
Shotke

1966

President Thomas C. Eley
1st Vice President Dr. Robert R. J.
Hilker
2nd Vice President Franz Altschuler
Secretary Mrs. S. J. Palormo
Treasurer David L. Soltker
Directors Mrs. Thomas A. Griffen,
Richard Shotke, Leigh
Sills, William Swan,
Helen M. Toussaint, Frank
M. Zeletz

1967

President Thomas C. Eley
1st VicePresident Dr. Robert R. J. Hilker
2nd Vice President David L. Soltker
Secretary Mrs. Samuel Palormo
Treasurer Gabe Burton
Directors: Mrs. O. M. Forkert, Arnold Besse, Leigh Sills, William D. Swan, Jr., Helen M. Toussaint, Frank M. Zeletz

1969

President Mrs. O. M. Forkert
1st Vice President John B. Cashion
2nd Vice President James G. Donegan
Secretary Mrs. Don Kron
Treasurer Gabe W. Burton
Directors Arnold E. Besse, A. B. Cassettari, Martha David, James L. Garner, Richard J. Hoerger, David L. Watt

1970-71

President James G. Donegan
1st Vice President Alan Rappaport
2nd Vice President David R. Vopatek
Secretary Mrs. Don Kron
Treasurer Edward Vardon
Directors A. B. Cassettari, Martha David, Richard J. Hoerger, Daniel N. Parker, David L. Watt, Dr. Patricia Yeoman

1972-73

President Alan Rappaport
1st Vice President David Vopatek
2nd Vice President Frank Blatchford, III
Secretary Frances Snow
Treasurer Charles Shea
Directors Ruth Aten, Martha David, Vincent Getzendanner, Roger Kiley, Jr., David L. Watt, Dr. Patricia Yeoman

1974

President Robert A. Davidson
1st Vice President Edward Klinenberg
Secretary Elizabeth Baby
Treasurer Charles M. Shea
Directors Paul Fahrenkrog, Gregory H. Furda, Barbara Frietsch, Hannah Sue Samuels, David Vopatek, Mary Jane Wiesinger

1975

President Edward L. Klinenberg
1st Vice President Frances S. Snow
2nd Vice President Richard K. Means
Secretary Suzanne E. Wren
Treasurer Robert B. George
Directors Charles J. Barnhill, Paul Fahrenkrog, Barbara Frietsch, Gregory H. Furda, Timothy J. Riordan, Hannah Sue Samuels

1976

President Maurice Forkert
1st Vice President Gregory L. Furda
2nd Vice President Richard K. Means
Secretary Carol Graham
Treasurer Robert B. George
Directors Charles G. Barnhill, Paul
Fahrenkrog, Barbara
Frietsch, Timothy J.
Riordan, Hannah Sue
Samuels, Leigh Sills

1977

President Maurice Forkekrt
1st Vice President Richard K. Means
2nd Vice President Carol Graham
Secretary Sunnie Olson
Treasurer Leigh Sills
Directors Henry Baby, Charles
Barnhill, Sheldon Beugen,
James Dupree, Paul
Fahrenkrog, Christopher
Middleton

1978

President Carol Graham
1st Vice President H. Sue Samuels
2nd Vice President Henry Baby
Secretary Barbara Mason
Treasurer Paul Kuhn
Directors Sheldon Beugen, Larry
Blust, Paul Fahrenkrog,
Christopher Middleton,
Father Don Miller, Sunnie
Olson

1979

President Paul H. Kuhn
1st Vice President H. Sue Samuels
2nd Vice President Larry Blust
Secretary Donna McLean
Treasurer Howard J. Bolnick
Directors Elizabeth Barnhill, Shel
Beugen, Roger E. Kaplan,
Donald A. Neltnor, Jim
Ryser, Joyce White

1980

President Elizabeth Barnhill
1st Vice President Irma Blatchford
2nd Vice President Walter Netsch
Secretary Marita Thompson
Treasurer Mike Marget
Directors Larry Blust, Richard
DuFour, Fred Henry,
Roger Kaplan, Donald A.
Neltnor

1981

President Elizabeth Barnhill
1st Vice President Larry Blust
2nd Vice President Richard DuFour
Secretary Marita Thompson
Treasurer Dorn Dean
Directors Norman Baugher, Jerrie
Boyle, Fred Henry, Roger
E. Kaplan, Jim Ryser,
Barry Soloff

1982

President Larry Blust
1st Vice President Dick DuFour
2nd Vice President Barry Soloff
Secretary Betty Fromm
Treasurer Dan Orzechowski
Directors Jerri Boyle, Fred Henry, Scott Cummings, Jim Ryser, Susan Morley Whipple, Mary Gehr Ray

1983

President Hannah Sue Samuels
1st Vice President Fred Henry
2nd Vice President Gail Rietze
Secretary Betty Fromm
Treasurer Allan Swaringen
Directors Scott Cummings, Carol Ovitz Hancock, John O'Callaghan, Mary Gehr Ray, Jim Ryser, Terry Sullivan

1984

President Fred Henry
1st Vice President John O'Callaghan
2nd Vice President Betty Fromm
Secretary Cynthia Knochel
Treasurer Myron Cholden
Directors Monika Betts, Carol Ovitz Hancock, Bill Leslie, Mary Gehr Ray, Hannah Sue Samuels, Terry Sullivan

1985

President Betty Fromm
1st Vice President Dick DuFour
2nd Vice President Carol Ovitz Hancock
Secretary Herbert Fisher
Treasurer Donald Neltnor
Directors Monika Betts, J. Allen Carley, Myron Cholden, Michael Kralovec, David Maytnier, Hannah Sue Samuels

1986

President Betty Fromm
1st Vice President David Maytnier
2nd Vice President John L. Huff
Secretary Herbert Fisher
Treasurer Donald Neltnor
Directors Monika Betts, J. Allen Carley, Myron Cholden, Lark Hapke, Bruno Ast, Tom Garvey

1987

President Bruno Ast
1st Vice President Sheldon Beugen
2nd Vice President Herbert Fisher
Secretary Ann Ferguson
Treasurer Donald Neltnor
Directors Betty Fromm, John L. Huff, Daniel W. Weil, Tom Garvey, J. Allen Carley, Lark J. Hapke

1988

President Bruno Ast
1st Vice President Ann Ferguson
2nd Vice President Herbert Fisher
Secretary Dawn Keating
Treasurer Ron Adilman
Directors Larry Blust, Cindy
O'Callaghan, J. Allen
Carley, Betty Fromm, Tom
Garvey, Daniel W. Weil

1989

President Monika Betts
1st Vice President Ann T. Ferguson
2nd Vice President John A. Bross, Jr.
Secretary Penny Miller
Treasurer Ron Adilman
Directors Ben Beiler, Rick Herrick,
Larry Blust, Cindy
O'Callaghan, Betty
Fromm, Roger Skolnik

1990

President Monika Betts
1st Vice President John Bross
2nd Vice President Larry Blust
Secretary Ron Adilman
Treasurer Gary Lawson
Directors Ben Beiler, Diane
Gonzalez, Rick Herrick,
Cindy O'Callaghan,
Justine Price, Roger
Skolnik

1991

President Roger Skolnik
1st Vice President John Bross
2nd Vice President Larry Blust
Secretary Rick Herrick
Treasurer Gary Lawson
Directors Ben Beiler, Monika Betts,
Carolyn Davis, Scott Early,
Diane Gonzalez, Justine
Price

1992

President Roger Skolnik
1st Vice President Carol Gregg
2nd Vice President Pat French
Secretary Shirley Baugher
Treasurer Dan Baldwin
Directors John Bross, Carolyn Davis,
Scott Early, Diane
Gonzalez, Richard Holt,
Justine Price

1993

President Shirley Baugher
1st Vice President Carol Gregg
2nd Vice President Pat French
Secretary Linda Sarley
Treasurer Dan Baldwin
Directors Carolyn Davis, Diane
Gonzalez, Richard Holt,
Justine Price, Roger
Skolnik, Ruth Ann
Watkins

1994

President Shirley Baugher
1st Vice President Dan Baldwin
2nd Vice President Justine Price
Secretary Marilyn Swanson
Treasurer Scott Early
Directors Diane Gonzalez, Ann
Haule, Richard Holt, John
Mark Horton, Chris
Middleton, Ruth Ann
Watkins

1995

President Shirley Baugher
1st Vice President Dan Baldwin
2nd Vice President Justine Price
Secretary Marilyn Swanson
Treasurer Scott Early
Directors Sarah Bartlett, Mitchell
Cobey, Diane Gonzalez,
Rick Greenwood, Ann
Haule, Ruth Ann Watkins

1996

President Dan Baldwin
1st Vice President Scott Early
2nd Vice President Trinda Gray
O'Connor
Secretary Mary Morony
Treasurer Rick Greenwood
Directors Sarah Bartlett, Mitchell
Cobey, Fern Bomchill
Davis, Diane Gonzalez,
Mary Jo Robling, Marilyn
Swanson

1997

President Dan Baldwin
1st Vice President Scott Early
2nd Vice President Trinda Gray
O'Connor
Secretary Mary Morony
Treasurer Rick Greenwood
Directors Mitchell Cobey, Fern
Bomchill Davis, Diane
Gonzalez, Mary Jo
Robling, Marilyn
Swanson, Jan Whyte

1998

President Scott Early
1st Vice President Rick Greenwood
2nd Vice President Norman Baugher
Secretary Mary Morony
Treasurer Mitchell Cobey
Directors Dan Burdick, Fern
Bomchill Davis, Diane
Gonzalez, Phyllis Hall,
Sharon O'Brien, Mary Jo
Robling

1999

President Scott Early
1st Vice President Rick Greenwood
2nd Vice President Norman Baugher
Secretary Mary Morony
Treasurer Mitchell Cobey
Directors Dan Burdick, Fern
Bomchill Davis, Diane
Gonzalez, Phyllis Hall,
Sharon O'Brien, Mary Jo
Robling

2000

President Rick Greenwood
1st Vice President Dan Baldwin
2nd Vice President Carolyn Blackmon
Secretary Linda Miller
Treasurer Tim Westerbeck
Directors Dan Burdick, Fern
    Bomchill Davis, Phyllis
    Hall, Carol Ovitz
    Hancock, Sharon O'Brien,
    Patricia Russell

2001

President Rick Greenwood
1st Vice President Dan Burdick
2nd Vice President Carolyn Blackmon
Secretary Linda Miller
Treasurer Dan Baldwin
Directors Fern Bomchill Davis, Lee
    Freidheim, Phyllis Hall,
    Carol Ovitz Hancock,
    Marshall Marcus, Patricia
    Russell

Old Town Triangle Association Officers and Board of Directors 2001

Officers

President Rick Greenwood
1st Vice-President Dan Burdick
2nd Vice-President Carolyn Blackmon
Secretary Linda Miller
Treasurer Dan Baldwin

Board of Directors

Fern Bomchill Davis
Lee Freidheim
Phyllis Hall
Carol Ovitz Hancock
Marshall Marcus
Patricia Russell

BACK, LEFT TO RIGHT: HANCOCK, BLACKMON, FREIDHEIM, BURDICK
FRONT, LEFT TO RIGHT: MARCUS, RUSSELL, GREENWOOD, WIZARD, BALDWIN, HALL.
DAVIS AND MILLER NOT SHOWN

Lucy Baldwin

Criteria for Designation of Chicago Landmarks

In reviewing a building or district for landmark designation, the Commission on Chicago Landmarks, a nine-member board appointed by the mayor, considers the seven criteria outlined in the Municipal Code of Chicago:

» Its value as an example of the architectural, cultural, economic, historic, social, or other aspect of the heritage of the City of Chicago, State of Illinois, or the United States

» Its location as a site of a significant historical event

» Its identification with a person or persons who significantly contributed to the culture and development of the City of Chicago

» Its exemplification of the cultural, economic, social, or historic heritage of the City of Chicago

» Its portrayal of the environment of a group of people in an era of history characterized by a distinctive architectural style

» Its embodiment of distinguishing characteristics of an architectural type or specimen

» Its identification as the work of an architect or master builder whose individual work has influenced the development of the City of Chicago

» Its embodiment of elements of architectural design, detail, materials, or craftsmanship which represent a significant architectural innovation

» Its relationship to other distinctive areas which are eligible for preservation according to a plan based on an historic, cultural, or architectural motif

» Its unique location or singular physical characteristic representing an established and familiar visual feature of a neighborhood, community, or the City of Chicago

The Designation Process

» Request for local landmark designation. Buildings or districts can be recommended for designation by members of the public, civic groups, or staff of the Commission on Chicago Landmarks.

» Work program set by the Commission. Each fall, the Commission establishes a work plan (five to ten designations) for the coming year. The plan is based on previous recommendations.

» Designation by Commission staff. Staff researches historic and architectural significance of properties on the work plan; submits report to the Commission.

» Preliminary determination of eligibility. Commission votes on whether to proceed with the designation. A positive vote gives the Commission authority to review building permits during the designation process.

» Report from the Department of Planning and Development. Statement of how the proposed landmark designation fits with neighborhood plans and policies.

» Commission request for owner's consent. The owner's consent is advisory—not required—for designation. When there is a nonconsenting response, a public hearing is required.

» Final recommendation. After a review of the designation record, the Commission votes whether to recommend designation to the City.

» Hearing by the City Council's Landmarks Committee. The Commission's recommendation is referred to the Committee on Historical Landmarks Preservation, which votes whether to recommend the designation to the City Council.

» Designation vote by the City Council. Designation of a Chicago Landmark is a legislative act of the Chicago City Council.

National Register of Historic Places Criteria

The National Register of Historic Places is the list of buildings, districts, sites, structures, or objects that are considered historically, architecturally, or archaeologically significant and worthy of preservation. Although the National Register is maintained by the U. S. Department of the Interior, nominations for Illinois properties are processed by the Illinois Historic Preservation Agency. According to the agency, a building, district, or site must:

» Be associated with events that have made a significant contribution to the broad patterns of history

» Be associated with the lives of significant persons in our past

» Be distinctive for its type, period, and method of construction; or represent the work of a master, or possess artistic value; or, in the case of a district, be representative of a significant and distinguishable entity whose components may lack individual distinction

» Yield important information about the area's history

National Register Process

» The Illinois Preservation Agency processes applications for the National Register of Historic Places. The four-step process includes: preliminary staff review, submission of the National Register form, review of the property on the basis of National Register criteria, and recommendation on the application.

» After the applicant has submitted information and photos of the property, the Illinois Historic Preservation Agency's National Register staff evaluates the property's significance and integrity.

» After the evaluation, staff sends a written opinion to the applicant. If the opinion is positive, a nomination form is sent to the applicant. If the opinion is negative, staff will advise the applicant of criteria issues that should be addressed.

» Following the receipt of the form, the property is considered at the next meeting of the Illinois Historic Sites Advisory Council.

» If the property is within a certified local government, the nomination will be forwarded to the community for its official comment on the listing.

» The 15-member advisory council evaluates the property in terms of the National Register criteria, then votes whether to recommend the nomination.

» A positive vote by the Council sends the nomination to the State Historic Preservation Officer of the Department of the Interior, who is the one to officially nominate the structure or district.

» The nomination is sent to the Keeper of the National Register Coordinator at the Illinois Historic Preservation Agency.

BIBLIOGRAPHY

Books

Bach, I.J., Wolfson, S. (1994). *Chicago on foot*. Chicago: Chicago Review Press

Bernstein, A. (1998). *Hollywood on Lake Michigan*. Chicago: Lake Claremont Press

Cromie, R. (1994). *The great Chicago fire*. Nashville: Rutledge Hill Press

Cronin, W. (1991). *Nature's metropolis*. New York: W.W. Norton & Company

Dell, A. (ed.). (2000). *20th century Chicago*. Chicago: Sports Publishing Inc.

Gonzalez, Diane, et. al. (1999). *50 years and counting*. Chicago: Old Town Triangle Association

Hucke, Matt & Ursula Bielski. (1999). *Graveyards of Chicago*. Chicago: Lake Claremont Press

Liebling, A. J. (1952). *Chicago, the second city*. New York: Alfred A. Knopf

Lowe, D.G. (2000) *Lost Chicago*. New York: Watson-Guptill Publications

Lowe, David. (1979). *The great Chicago fire*. New York: Dover Publications, Inc.

Sawyers, June Skinner (1991). *Chicago portraits*. Chicago: Loyola University Press

Sinkevitch, A. ed. (1993). *AIA guide to Chicago*. New York: Harcourt Brace & Co.

Spinney, R. G. (2000). *City of big shoulders*. DeKalb: Northern Illinois University Press

Watt, D. & L. eds. (1971) *Chicago 1871*. Chicago: Old Town Triangle Association

Art Fair Program Books

Angle, P.M. (1954). Home sweet home

Angle, P. (1956). The bells of St.Michael's

Angle, P. (1961). Old Town days

Angle, P. (1959). The art fair and how it grew

Beverly, J. (1953). This is Old Town

Clayton, H. (1953). Chicago's left bank

Cook, J. (1953). The Menomonee Club

Cook, J. (1954). Old Town—future

Emmons, et al. eds. (1952). A neighborhood portrait

Emmons, P.W. (1953). Zahner park

Forkert, L.D.S. (1953). The old burying ground

Forkert, A. (1978). The unknown Old Town triangle

Forkert, M. (1976). Lest we forget

Goldstein, S. & D. (1965). Old Town architecture

Guilbert, H. (1953). Old Town gardens

Herbert, D. (1954). Old Town—present

Holabird, J. (1964). Old Town architecture

Hyer, W.G. (1961). The Menomonee club

Hyer, W.G. (1986). The Old Town triangle: a brief look back

Kogan, H. (1959). A sense of history, more or less

Kogan, H. (1969). A quick history & some trivia

Leonard, W. (1954). Three-sided and two-speeded

Morris, E. (1961). Life and legend in Old Town

Morris, E. (1961). A round dozen holidays

Murray, G. (1958). Old Town, the pickle, and the wobs

Norris, H. (1970). What to write for the Old Town art fair catalogue

Porterfield, C. (1966). Old Town: A view from the back porch

Reddy, J. (1971). St. Michael's and the great Chicago fire

Reed, E. (1953). The triangle look

Schnedeker, J. (1962). What is Old Town?

Sills, L. (1975). A Frenchman at the heart of the triangle

Watt. D.L. (1966). 1966 and all that

Weissenborn, L.J. (1954). Here is Old Town–past

Wells, S. (1964). Francis Chapin, man of good will

Whybrow, D. (1974). Living in the triangle

(1960). 1851 and all that—or the birth and christening of Old Town (author unlisted)

(1987). Bill Hanselman's chairs and the great Chicago fire (author unlisted)

(1990). 41st Old Town Art Fair: a self guided tour to some points of historic and architectural interest. (author unlisted)

Other

Kelly, W. (1964). "Old Town, from farming celery to farming money." Kenilworth: *Omnibus*, pp. 39-43

Kristak, S. (1997). "The new Old Town." Chicago: *Echo*, Nov. 13

Rand, L. (1987). "Walking tour of Old Town." *In Chicago*, pp. 4-8.

Suchar, C. (1984). "Icons of civility: the changing face of the Lincoln Park neighborhood." Chicago: *DePaul University Chicago Area Studies Center*

Newspapers

Angle, P.M. (1961). "Old Town." *Chicago Sun Times Midwest Magazine*, June 4.

Blair, S. (1963). "Beauty blooms in a run-down area," *Chicago American*, Jan. 29

Browning, N.L. (1957). "Let's tour Old Town." *Chicago Tribune*, December 1.

Collin, D. (1965). "Will success spoil Old Town," *Chicago Tribune*, Dec. 12.

Gill, D. (1967). "Battle of the high rise," *Chicago Tribune*, Dec. 6.

Hill, L. (1989). "Lincoln Park wasn't always upscale", *Skyline*, March 9.

Hunt, R. (1964). "Savoring Wells street." *Chicago Tribune*, June 7.

Jiminez, G. (1985). "Old Town's ups and downs," *Chicago Sun Times*, Feb. 1.

Kufrin, J. (1964). "I remember Wells street," *Chicago Daily News*, October 17

Lee, V. (1963). "The happy faces of Crilly court ," *Chicago American*, March 10

Lyon, M. (1952). "There are no squares in Old Town's triangle," *Chicago Tribune*, Nov. 22.

Stracke, W. (1971). "The joyous noise of Old Town," *Chicago Tribune Magazine*, Dec. 26.

Miscellaneous History

Hill, L. (1990). The history of Old Town through the headlines. Oral presentation at Old Town Triangle Association's Annual Meeting

Weissenborn, L.J. (1955). "Old Town in retrospect," *unpublished manuscript*, gift to Chicago Historical Society

Chicago Commission on Landmarks (2001). unpublished manuscript, research on residence at 1710 Crilly Court for Landmarks designation

Landis, D. (1961). Letter to Mr. D. E. Mackelman, Commissioner Community Conservation Board re: General Neighborhood Renewal Plan for the Triangle

Durkott, J. et.al. eds. (1988). "A History of the Old Town Triangle" (transcript of partially completed oral history project)

INDEX

PHOTOGRAPHS BY PAGE NUMBERS

AUTHOR

Shirley Baugher, a resident of the Old Town Triangle since 1978, received her MA and Ph.D in history from Northwestern University. She has written many American history texts for elementary and high school students. She was president of the Old Town Triangle Association for three years and currently works at the Triangle Center as an administrator.

PHOTO RESEARCHER

As chair of the education department for the Field Museum of Natural History, Carolyn Blackmon developed the museum's first volunteer program; introduced adult education courses, performances, and environmental field trips; organized the outreach program for caregivers and children; expanded the loan center for teachers; and established family workshops and overnight events. She was involved in professional growth programs for museum staff nationwide. In 1992, she received the American Association of Museums Award for Excellence in Practice. Though she retired from the Field Museum in 1996, she continues to serve on numerous advisory committees and boards. Currently, she is active with the Old Town Triangle Association as Chair of the 2001 Art Fair and a member of the Historic District Planning & Zoning Committee.

TEXT AND COVER DESIGNER

Norman Baugher has created the Old Town Art Fair poster and program book covers since 1988. Among his many award-winning designs is the Millennium cover for World Book Encyclopedia. In 2000, he developed an image that has become the official logo for all Triangle publications.

EDITOR, PROOFREADER

Since moving to Old Town in 1979, Trinda Gray O'Connor has been an active neighborhood resident. She served as General Chair of the Old Town Art Fair in 1996 and 1997 and continues to volunteer her time and skills on Art Fair committees. As an independent consultant to associations, Ms. Gray O'Connor specializes in event planning, project management, administration, and print services.

COVER ARTIST

Norman Zimmerman is a longtime resident of Old Town, so long, in fact, that his memory has faded. He recalls nothing of his former life. Rumor has it, however, that he is an architect working on his MFA at the Old Town Art School, majoring in water color painting. He aspires to create a really scary sky